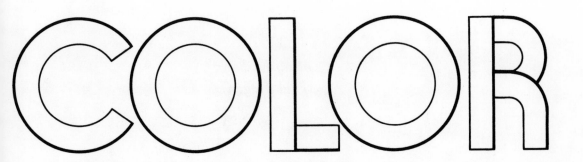

COLOR

A GUIDE FOR EVERY PAINTER

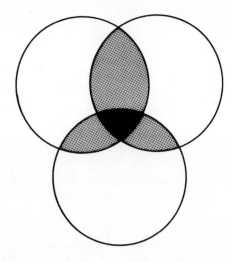

Catherine Hagen

To my husband
Paul Hagen

Library of Congress Cataloging in Publication Data

Hagen, Catherine.
Color: a guide for every painter.

SUMMARY: *Lessons and exercises in color principles designed*
to build memory patterns in students
which will enable them to produce predictable color.
1. Colors. [1. Colors] I. Title.
ND1510.H33   751.4'5   75–43035
ISBN 0–8098–5002–8

Manufactured in the United States of America
Designed by The Etheredges

Acknowledgments

It is impossible to thank all who have helped me in the realization of this work. However, there are those whose names I must mention.

I have been blessed with an understanding husband, Paul Hagen, who, though not an artist, has contended with art and been patient with artists. To him I give my deepest gratitude for his encouragement and help in every detail of this book.

I owe a debt of gratitude to Flora North, president of Howell-North Books. The idea of writing a book did not come into focus until Flora, a student in my color class, urged me to put my lessons into book form. I am grateful for her inspiration and guidance.

To my editor, Lorna Greenberg, I extend sincere thanks for her generous help in the preparation and organization of this work.

I extend grateful appreciation to Robert Arrowood of San Francisco, who so generously made the beautiful transparencies for the color plates.

For their warm interest I wish to thank dear friends, Ruth and Dewey Coleman, in whose studio I have conducted my art classes.

I wish to express my loving gratitude to my sister, Frances Barragar, for her interest in my art work through the years, and for her constant encouragement.

In a very special way I thank Marjorie Cathcart, Avis DeMonte, Ruth Duhring, Eleanor Elsocht, Robert Elsocht and Janet Langmaid, all prize-winning artists, who studied color with me. I am grateful for their inspiration and enthusiastic support.

My sincere thanks go to Catherine De Lucchi Kelly, young art student, for her inspiration as well as valuable assistance with reading and typing; and to Jeri Porterfield, who assisted me with the final editorial revision of the text.

I am grateful to Constance Hall for her help on the diagrams, and to Helen Menton and my niece, Catherine Moloney, for checking the text and carrying out work on the assignments. Many thanks to Irene Hagen, Peggy Moloney, Sigrid Menton and Connie Flaherty for typing and proofreading the manuscript.

CATHERINE HAGEN

Contents

EXPANDING THE PRIMARIES

INTRODUCING ANALOGOUS COLOR

BEFORE YOU BEGIN

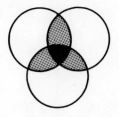

Introduction

As a teacher observing the work of beginning painters and gifted amateur painters, I saw too many paintings start with joyous color and end in a sea of green mud. I also saw paintings with fine color relationships which the artist could never repeat because they were accidental.

Some students felt that a precise study of color was too slow, and that they could solve their problems through trial and error. Others seemed to feel that through happy accident, they could get by, or that whatever they did was exceptional merely because it was original. The majority of students, eager to learn and willing to work, found that most color instruction, both in classes and in books, assumed a basic knowledge of color. They were left with many unrelated recipes for certain effects, but with nothing to build on.

Artists should be able to produce predictable color. This means that artists should be able, upon viewing a color—green, for instance—

to know whether it is a pure green from a tube, or a mixture of yellow and blue. They should know which yellow and which blue, of all the available yellows and blues, were used to make this green. Further, they should be able to glance at some yellow paint and some blue paint placed side-by-side and know exactly what kind of green these colors would produce if mixed. And even further, artists should be able to visualize what the tints of the green would look like, and how the green would appear if grayed by its complementary.

In my search for a way to help student painters acquire this kind of knowledge, I concluded that the only answer was to go back to the primary colors. The way is so clear and uncluttered, and the addition of new colors grows naturally from this beginning. The next step was to decide on a painting material suitable for teaching color, which would also be a material easily handled by students.

The most commonly used types of paint are watercolor paint, acrylic paint and oil paint. With watercolor it is difficult to explain how much water is picked up by the brush. Since a combination of two or more colors is mixed on the brush by dipping a wet brush into one color and then into another, it is impossible to describe an exact quantity measurement of paint. I find that an in-depth study of color is too difficult with this kind of water-based paint.

Acrylic paint has a very rapid drying quality, sometimes drying in seconds after being exposed to the air. This condition makes a careful mixing and analysis of each color almost impossible.

My conclusion that oil paint is the most suitable material for teaching and learning about color was made for several reasons, the most important of which was its color constancy. Watercolor paint tends to lighten as it dries on paper, while acrylic paint darkens in drying on the canvas. With oil paints, the color that the students mix on the palette is that identical color after it is placed on the canvas and dries. Also oil paint dries slowly, giving students time to observe the changes in colors as they mix them with a palette knife on the palette. The very bulk of the material makes it pleasant to manipulate with a palette knife. Oil paint can be squeezed onto the palette in almost the exact amount desired. It can also be divided into portions on the palette, and the colors can be moved from one place to another on the palette without too much loss of paint.

The principles contained in these lessons can be applied to water-color, acrylic, or any other painting medium.

Taking a year away from teaching, I developed a series of color lessons starting with the primary colors: red, yellow and blue. Each lesson produces a memory pattern which can be expanded to include any of the wide range of colors now available.

Even though I have included short excursions into composition and other elements of painting, this book does not pretend to teach painting technique. I have detailed the lessons exactly as I teach them. The students learn to produce predictable color, but the manner of placing color on the canvas, the brushwork, and the subject matter remain their own.

I have tried to arrange these lessons and exercises in a logical order so that the student will build a memory pattern of first principles. I will not promise that you will become a famous artist, but I can promise that these first principles will be as valuable to you as the alphabet is to the writer—something you know so well that you forget you know it.

Comment on Color

Many books have been written on the subject of color, but they frequently treat the theory of light only. Light itself is invisible, yet it contains all color. We see only the reflected light from the surface of objects on which the light ray falls. The object absorbs some of the colors of the light ray, and we see only the remaining colors which are reflected to our eyes. This is true of every object that we view—flowers, trees, people—in fact, everything.

While a thorough knowledge of the theory of light is interesting and worth knowing, it is not absolutely necessary for the student of painting. The art student should know the principle of spectrum color.

When a ray of light passes through a triangular glass prism, the prism breaks up the light ray into its component parts and projects these colors onto a white surface as a wedge-shaped band of colors: red, orange, yellow, green, blue and purple. These are the spectrum colors that we see in the rainbow. The separation of the spectrum colors was discovered about 1660 by Sir Isaac Newton. There cannot be a greater variety of colors than that found in the visible rays of the spectrum band.

Red, yellow and blue are known as primary colors because no combination of other colors can make a red, no combination of other colors can make a yellow, and no combination of other colors can make a blue.

In the spectrum, red mixes with yellow to form orange; yellow mixes with blue to form green; and blue mixes with red to form purple.

The eye focuses on the color red in such a way that we see red as if it were nearer to us than it actually is. Red is an advancing color. The eye focuses on blue in such a way that we see the color blue as if it were farther away than it actually is. Blue is a retreating color; it seems to move away. If one looks at an area of red on a blue background, there is a sense of vibrating or moving color, because the muscles of the eye contract and expand in an effort to focus on these two colors at the same time. The eye focuses normally on yellow, which neither retreats nor advances.

Artists call some colors warm, and other colors cool. Red and yellow, the colors we associate with fire, are warm. Blue, the color of the sky, of water and ice, is cool. There are cool reds because they contain a small amount of blue, just as there are warm blues containing a small amount of red.

The eye seems to demand all the colors in light. It is a physical fact. When a color is absent, the eye supplies it. If you stare at an area of red on a white background for a time, you begin to see a green glow around the red area. This is caused by the eye supplying the other two primary colors—yellow and blue.

Another example of the eye supplying the missing color is the "after image," which we all experience. This can be produced by staring at a brilliant color—blue for instance. When the eyes are immediately closed, the color orange will be seen. It is a combination of the missing red and yellow.

Still another example is demonstrated by staring at a burning light bulb, normally yellow. Close your eyes and you will see the shape of the bulb, but it will appear violet, which is a tint of purple (red and blue combined). The colors thus supplied by the eye are said to be complementary colors, because they complete the spectrum.

The complementary of red is green, and in reverse the complementary of green is red. The complementary of yellow is purple, and in reverse the complementary of purple is yellow. The complementary of blue is orange, and in reverse the complementary of orange is blue.

Pigment color begins as a powder of mineral, vegetable or chemical origin. When this colored powder is mixed with a binder, we have paint.

The binder for watercolor paint is gum arabic. The binder for acrylic paint is acrylic-polymer emulsion. For oil paint, the colored powder is ground in one of the drying oils—usually linseed oil. There are other forms of painting materials, but these three are most commonly used.

We cannot duplicate the purity and brilliance of the colors in light rays, but we can interpret our world as we see it with the many beautiful colors in oil paint that we have today.

Primitive artists had only four colors, red earth, yellow earth, charcoal and chalk. They probably used grease as a binder. We use these same earth colors today.

Today's artists with their wealth of pigment colors need not feel sorry for the artists of the stone age, with their four colors. The remarkable paintings in the caves of France and Spain have lasted for thousands of years.

The Color Wheel

Nearly eighteen hundred years ago, around the year 200, the astronomer Ptolemy devised a color wheel. All knowledge of this was lost for centuries, until 1660 when Sir Isaac Newton developed a similar idea. These scientists were dealing with the colors in light rays.

Sir Isaac Newton also conceived the idea of bending the spectrum band to form a circle. This is the basis of the color wheel, which we reproduce as closely as we can with our pigment colors.

Since Newton, the art student has been required to paint the spectrum colors in a careful and mechanically drawn circle, with box-like compartments for the colors. Measuring and drawing the shapes takes so much effort that the student is tired by the time the color is to be applied. I do not ask students to make this type of color wheel. I hope to teach them to "think" a color wheel, which in my experience is the best way of teaching color.

At the beginning of each lesson in this book you will draw a pencil circle about six inches in diameter. Keep it as round as possible, but don't worry about it. This circle represents the color wheel.

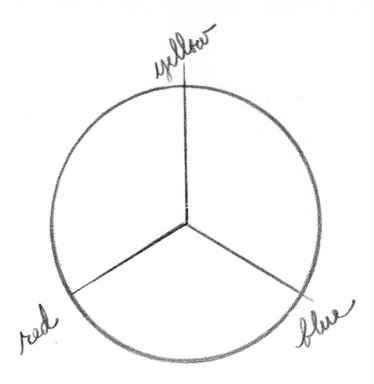

On the circle, place three pencil marks to divide it into three equal parts; one mark at the left, one mark at the top, and one mark at the right. Try to be careful with the divisions.

Next to the mark on the left write the word red, and visualize the color red as you write it. At the top of the circle write the word yellow, and visualize yellow as you write it. At the mark on the right place the word blue, and visualize the color blue as you write. These are the primary colors. For identification we call this the Common Triad. (A triad means a group of three.)

Red is the first color in the spectrum band, and since we read from left to right, red is placed at the left on the color wheel.

In the spectrum the primary colors overlap and blend with each other, thus forming secondary colors.

Halfway between the red and yellow on the pencil wheel, place a mark and name it orange. Visualize the color orange. Halfway between yellow and blue place a mark and name it green, visualizing the color green. At the bottom of the circle, between blue and red, place a mark and name it purple, visualizing the color purple.

Looking at the color wheel you will observe that the complementary colors are opposite each other on a straight line drawn through the center of the circle.

From the colors in the Common Triad you will produce many new, distinct and beautiful colors. Later you will create new triads from other reds, other yellows and other blues. All the colors produced by the new triads will be different. But the same principle holds true, because you will be following one of nature's laws—that of the spectrum.

The Common Triad

The three basic colors of the spectrum, red, yellow and blue, can only be approximated by pigment color. Since we shall refer to these frequently, we will call them a triad. I think it important to repeat this fact: these are called primary colors because no combination of colors can make a red; no combination of colors can make a yellow; no combination of colors can make a blue.

The purest red color contains some yellow and blue; the purest yellow color contains some blue and red; and the purest blue color contains some red and yellow.

For the basic pigment triad, I have chosen cadmium red light, cadmium yellow light and ultramarine blue because of all the available colors, these contain the least of the other two colors.

This triad will be known as the Common Triad. In later studies the student will create other triads—each of which will consist of one red color, one yellow color and one blue color.

The first five lessons in this book will be devoted to a development of the Common Triad. The principles involved are most important, and will govern all of the various reds, yellows and blues which the student will encounter in the future.

The Painter's Vocabulary

There are certain words in the artist's vocabulary which the beginning painter may not understand. Then there are also some familiar words to which the artist gives special meaning. Such a word is "hue." One meaning is a color—red hue, yellow hue, blue hue. It can mean more than that, however. It can mean a color's redness, its yellowness or its blueness. To avoid confusion, I will use the word sparingly and the meaning will always be the redness, the yellowness or the blueness of a color.

Some descriptive words in our vocabulary are overworked and precise meanings overlooked. The word "strong" is one of these. We say, a strong breeze, strong coffee, strong chair, strong odor, strong brush stroke, and of course, strong color. In this book I will use the word strong in relation to the pigment as it comes from the tube—for example, cadmium red light is a strong pigment color; cadmium yellow light is a weak pigment color. If equal amounts of these two pigment colors are mixed together on the palette with a palette knife, the red color over-powers the yellow color which completely disappears. Ultramarine blue is also a strong pigment color, but not as strong as cadmium red light.

When I describe a color painted on a canvas or seen in a painting, I may describe it as intense, vibrant, or brilliant, but never as a "strong" color.

The word "shade" is often used as a substitute for the word "value." In the dictionary the word value means a measurement of some kind. In the artist's vocabulary the word value is a measurement of the amount of light that a color contains.

The word shade has many meanings: the shade cast by a tree, a window shade, a shade of meaning. Shakespeare writes of a ghost as a shade. Comparative darkness is sometimes called shade. A degree of color is a shade—such as, a shade of green. And finally a degree of gray somewhere between black and white is called a shade.

Due to these divergent meanings, I will avoid the word "shade" in this book. When a degree of light in any color is designated, it will always be referred to as the "value" of that color, not a shade.

Materials

PAINTS

Oil paint is available in the widest variety of colors; but to begin the study of color, we will use only the three basic colors of the spectrum.

I have chosen cadmium red light, cadmium yellow light and ultramarine blue for the first five lessons. In my experience these colors retain their purity and brilliance after being mixed one with another to produce the twelve intervals of color which we use. The student will also need one large (one pound) tube of zinc, or titanium white. Lead white or flake white (also lead) are not as commonly used because they tend to yellow when stored away from the light.

The tube colors I have chosen for lessons six through twelve are listed below. For the students' individual choice a more complete list of tube colors will be found in the chapters on "Warm and Cool Colors" and "Transparent And Opaque Colors."

Oil paint comes in tubes of three sizes. I suggest that the beginning student buy the cadmium red light and the ultramarine blue in medium-size tubes, about four inches long and one inch in diameter. For the cadmium yellow light a large tube, about eight inches long and two inches in diameter, will be more economical because the yellow paint has a weaker pigment strength and is used up more rapidly.

I urge you to buy the best quality paint. In some of the cheaper brands of paint the actual color is not as good as that of top quality paint. Inexpensive paints sometimes contain an inert filler which dilutes the color intensity. Cadmium red light and cadmium yellow light are to be very carefully selected. If you have a choice between two different brands of these colors, ask the salesperson to remove the caps of the tubes so that you can compare the colors. Choose the red that has the least orange in it. The yellow too sometimes tends toward orange, which is not desirable. Ultramarine blue is usually a good color in any of the better brands of paint.

The tube colors must be chosen carefully because the success of your work depends on their selection.

Paints required for the first five lessons:

Cadmium red light
Cadmium yellow light
Ultramarine blue
Zinc white or titanium white

Paints required for lessons six through twelve:

Cadmium red light	Cadmium yellow light
Alizarin crimson	Cadmium yellow medium
Burnt sienna	Yellow ochre
Thalo red rose	Indian yellow
Scarlet	Cadmium orange
Acra red	
Cobalt violet	Ultramarine blue
	Thalo blue
	Cerulean blue
	Viridian green

Ultramarine violet
Ivory black

Zinc white or titanium white.

BRUSHES

I suggest that you have at least four good bristle brushes to start. The brush easiest to handle is a squarish one called a "bright." Another brush type is called a "flat." In the same size brush, the bristles of the flat are longer than those of the bright.

Numbers on brushes indicate their size. Number 1 is the smallest, and the numbers continue consecutively to number 12, after which the sizes are numbered 14, 16, 18 and 20. Some brands of brushes are not numbered. Two of your brushes should be number 12, about one inch across the metal part of the brush. This metal part which holds the bristles together is called the ferrule. Your other two brushes should be larger, possibly a number 14 and a number 18. You may need one small brush, a number 6 perhaps; but it should be used only for sketching with paint.

You may want to try both types of brushes, the bright and the flat. They are equally good, and only you can decide which is best for you. I prefer the bright because it gives a broad brush stroke for large areas. It also gives a sharp edge or a clean line, if used sideways.

A teacher once told me that the best rule for choosing a brush for any size canvas is, "Use the largest brush possible. Using a small brush on a large canvas is as ineffectual as trying to wash an elephant with a toothbrush!"

When buying a brush, check to see that the bristles are thick near the ferrule. If there are too few bristles, the brush is flabby and useless. It should have a springy quality.

To clean a brush thoroughly while you are painting, wipe off as much paint as possible on a paint rag. Dip the brush into the turpentine (or paint thinner), but do not swish it around. Wipe again on the rag. Do this until fairly clean. Now put some white paint on the palette. Work the brush back and forth in the white paint until the color is forced out of the bristles near the ferrule. Wipe your brush and rinse again. Your brush should be clean. This method is especially good when you have a strong color like cadmium red or one of the thalo colors on your brush.

It is not necessary to have an absolutely clean brush for each color. It may save a little paint, but not that much. There are times when a color needs a clean brush. At other times, clean your brushes by wiping them thoroughly as you go.

At the end of the day wash your brushes with a good soap. An old-fashioned soap containing naphtha is the best for this purpose. Do not allow paint to collect at the top of the bristles near the metal.

For drying, place the brushes on a newspaper tilted slightly so that the water runs away from the ferrule. Do not stand the brush on its handle or on the bristle.

PALETTES

The artist needs some sort of smooth non-absorbent surface on which to squeeze paint from the tube.

Historically the palette was made of a lightweight hardwood. It was oval in shape and had a thumbhole at one end. The artist held it while working.

New materials are now available to replace the old wooden palette. I use large palettes made from baked enamel on masonite, that I purchase from a lumberyard. It is sold under different trade names; the one I use is called Marlite. It is available in large sheets that measure four feet by eight feet. For a small fee, it can be cut into fourteen palettes, each measuring sixteen by twenty inches.

When cut by a saw the edges are very rough and sharp. They should be sandpapered smooth and the corners trimmed at the same time.

Some artists find Formica a satisfactory material for a palette. It should be glued to a board because the material is rather thin and the edges sharp.

An inexpensive palette for home use can be made from a piece of glass (preferably plate glass) under which you have pasted white paper. The edges should be bound with adhesive tape to protect the hands.

Cellophane tape and masking tape are not adequate protection. The palette must always be white and at least sixteen by twenty inches in size.

PALETTE KNIVES

There are two types of palette knives, one with a flat spatula blade and one with a trowel-shaped blade. For mixing paint on the palette the spatula-shaped knife is required. The trowel-shaped knife, which has a bend in the blade, is a painting knife used to place paint directly on the canvas. This trowel-shaped knife comes in many sizes, from a tiny blade fastened to a long stem to a very large blade several inches long. Since we are doing brush painting at this time, the trowel-shaped knife is unsatisfactory.

Your spatula-shaped knife should have a blade about six inches long. Later, when you need large quantities of paint for a large canvas, you should increase the size of your knife.

Test the knife for a springy quality before you buy it. Press the rounded point of the blade against the tabletop to see where the blade bends or curves. It should be at about the halfway point. If it bends too near the handle, you will spend more time wiping your hands than mixing paint.

CANVAS

Oil paints adhere more readily to a rough surface. For this reason canvas, either cotton or linen, is commonly used. For the beginning student, commercially available canvas board is quite satisfactory.

Canvas board is a lightweight, sized canvas that is glued on a heavy cardboard called chipboard. The edges are neatly finished. Over a period of time the canvas board may bulge or become concave, even in a frame. It cannot be depended upon to keep a perfectly flat surface. "Sizing" is a pasty substance used as a filler, or stiffener, for canvas. Without it the oil paint sinks into and through the canvas, the colors blur and become unmanageable.

Painters who are more experienced may use stretched canvas, which is a heavily sized canvas stretched over a frame of stretcher bars. This canvas may be purchased by the yard—usually fifty inches wide—at an art supply store.

The stretcher bars may also be bought in lengths from about six inches to forty-eight inches. Both ends of each bar are tongue and groove, and the frame can be put together by hand. Care must be taken to see that the corners form a ninety-degree angle.

There is also an unsized canvas sold by the yard which can be put on the stretcher bars. As a sizing for raw canvas, I recommend ordinary white latex wall paint or white latex paint primer. These are easy to handle and dry quickly. At least two coats of this sizing should be applied, allowing drying-time between the coats.

Gesso, a well-known commercial sizing for canvas, is available. For the student it is somewhat expensive.

For the beginner the measurement of your canvas should be at least twenty by twenty-four inches. If you start painting small pictures, it is almost impossible to acquire the freedom one needs for oil painting. The beauty of oil painting lies in the richness of the areas and the variety of the brush strokes. This cannot be accomplished on a small canvas. You should plan to increase the size of your canvas as soon as you have developed an acquaintance with your colors.

If the canvas seems dry when you start to paint—especially canvas board—rub it with a cloth moistened with turpentine or thinner. This will allow the paint to move more freely over the surface of the canvas.

PAINTING MEDIUM

The term "medium" has a number of different meanings. First, it refers to the material with which the artist chooses to work. The artist works in the medium of oils or the medium of watercolors.

A second meaning is that of a solvent for paint. The solvent fluid is different for each type of paint.

Water is the solvent for watercolor paint. For acrylic paint, the solvent can be either water or a solution made with water and a small amount of acrylic polymer emulsion. Turpentine or mineral spirits (ordinary paint thinner) are the solvents for oil paint. Turpentine was once thought superior to paint thinner; however, they are now considered equally good. One of these or the other should be used to clean brushes as you work. They should not be used to extend the paint because they dissolve the binder which holds the pigment together. It is extremely dangerous to use these solvents near an open flame.

The third meaning of the word medium is: a formula consisting of varnish, oil and turpentine, or paint thinner. Some of the uses for the formula are described later in this book.

A popular formula now being used is one-third Damar varnish, one-third linseed oil and one-third turpentine. Many artists use this formula because they prefer the dull or matte finish that it produces. Damar varnish is available in a gloss finish as well as the matte finish.

A formula which was used centuries ago consisted of one-third copal varnish, one-third stand oil and one-third rectified turpentine. This is still an excellent formula today.

I prefer that beginning painters work with the oil paint as it comes directly from the tube in order to become acquainted with the texture and beauty of the pure paint.

EASELS

An easel is required to hold the canvas in an upright position. This gives the artist freedom of motion for brush strokes. The artist should stand at the easel while painting. Standing allows freedom to move away from the work to view it from a distance. A tall stool is a good substitute for standing since it provides elbowroom.

A small table at the side of the easel is used to hold the palette, an upright container for brushes, and a can for thinner or turpentine.

A good sturdy easel is important. A most desirable one is a heavy wooden easel with a ratchet with which one can raise or lower the canvas. It also provides a clamp for the top of the canvas, thus holding it firmly. The small folding easel available in most art stores is not heavy enough to withstand the pressure of a good firm brush stroke.

Many of my students make their own easels, buying the materials at a lumberyard.

If the beginning painter is unable to stand while painting, a table-top easel is available. A stool, rather than a chair, permits greater freedom of movement for the arms.

LIGHT

The best light for painting is in a room with windows or a skylight facing north. The north light changes very little during the daylight hours.

It is difficult to paint in a room with sunlight streaming in through the window. The light in the room is usually a cool light, while the sunlight is warm and distracting to the eye.

All artists cannot have studios with a north light, but we can regulate the light we do have. In my studio unbleached muslin curtains (bleached white by many washings) are drawn across the windows when the sunshine comes in. These curtains diffuse the sunlight and seem to improve the light throughout the room.

Painting at night presents a different problem. The light from an ordinary light bulb is yellow. This neutralizes the yellow color of your paint. Therefore, the artist tends to use more intense yellow paint in order to see it. The electric light affects all the colors slightly, especially those with which yellow is mixed. If you work regularly at night, you can become accustomed to this by reducing the amount of yellow color used. Always look at your painting the next day in daylight to see how you have handled the yellows.

If you wish to use fluorescent lighting, be sure to obtain advice from an expert in that field. There are several different colors in fluorescent tubes.

CLOTHES AND PAINT RAGS

The traditional painter's smock is poor protection. A large and loose knee-length apron with half-sleeves and tying at the back is better. Paints, oils, turpentine and paint thinner damage leather, so you should wear comfortable old shoes. For standing long hours at a time, I use a pair of exercise sandals with wooden soles.

The painter constantly wipes paint from the brush while working, so have plenty of rags on hand. These may be torn into small pieces so that each can be discarded as it is used. It is advisable to place a paper-bag liner into your wastebasket so that the wet rags do not rub off on the wastebasket. It is a good idea to have a small stack of newspapers nearby in case you knock over a can of turpentine or thinner. Newspaper is much more efficient at absorbing these materials than rags.

I never have enough rags, so I use tissues. Paper towels are useful but should be torn apart before you start to paint. It is distracting as well as time wasting to put down your brushes, pick up the roll, tear off a piece, put down the roll, and pick up your brush. Remember that painting time is precious.

PAINTING WITH COLOR

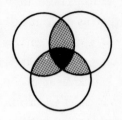

Lesson 1:
Values in Black and White

If we lived in a world which had light but no color, we would see everything we now see—houses, trees, flowers, people—but everything would be seen in terms of gray. Some objects would be light gray, some dark gray. Some objects would be white, others black. Objects would be seen only by the quantity of light they reflect. These measurements of light quantity are called "light values."

Since we live in a world of color, the value of a color is the amount of light that it contains. We tend to judge some colors as lighter than they actually are because of their warmth or brilliance. Because of the coolness of other colors, we judge them as darker than they really are. For this reason, we must understand values in black and white before trying to judge them in color. The color white reflects all color and it is the lightest value. The color black absorbs all color and it is the darkest value.

For the first four lessons, we use the three primary colors: cadmium red light, cadmium yellow light and ultramarine blue. These are the colors that are in white light. Theoretically, red plus yellow plus blue equals white light. Black absorbs all color, so it follows that red plus yellow plus blue also equals black.

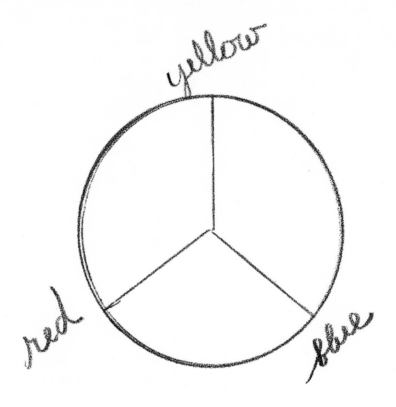

Our first problem is to produce black. Do not use a tube of black paint. Later we will discuss black tube paint and its use.

We should be able to measure out equal amounts of the three colors, mix them and produce black. However, the pigments differ in color strength. Cadmium red light is a very strong pigment color, and is also an intense and brilliant color on the canvas. Cadmium yellow light is a color of greater brilliance on the canvas, but as a pigment it is very weak compared with red. Ultramarine blue is a strong pigment color, but not as strong as red. It has a dark richness on the canvas. Because of the unequal strength of these pigments, we need different amounts of each.

Squeeze out three generous inches of ultramarine blue on the lower half of your palette. This is always the mixing area. Add about two inches of cadmium red light, and one inch of cadmium yellow light. Mix well with a palette knife. Don't mix the color by patting it. Lift it free from underneath and blend it—turn it over, trying to keep it somewhat together.

You will have a mass of paint of very dark value, but how do you know whether it is an exact black? There are some colors which are below the threshold of perception, just as there are sounds of music which are below the threshold of hearing. In music we can hear a very low sound, but we cannot tell whether it is a C or a D, or an X for that matter.

The mass of dark color which you have just mixed is below the threshold of sight. In order to bring the paint up to a value where you can judge the color, place a small amount on one side of the palette, and mix it with some white paint. Do not allow any white, or the test spot, to mix with the mass of black. If this test spot produces a true gray, it proves that your mass of color is a true black. If the sample gray is too blue, add very small amounts of red and yellow to the black. If the sample

gray seems too red, add very small amounts of blue and yellow to the black. If the sample gray seems green, add a small amount of red to the black. Test the mass of black again.

Early in my art training I learned that it is possible for the human eye to distinguish nine separate values from white to black. My students prove this every day. As an example, try this experiment in judging the values that surround you. Look around the room in which you are sitting, as I look around my room. In my room, the window curtains are white —value one. The walls are yellow—value number two; the seats of two chairs are a light green—a number three perhaps. A light-brown paper bag is number four. My typewriter is gray—value number five. The green carpet is darker than my typewriter—value number six. The sofa, blue and green, is next—value number seven. The walnut frames of the chairs are very dark but not as dark as black—they can be considered value number eight. My pencils are extremely dark blue, which I consider a nine value. Once aware of values, the student begins to enjoy small nuances of color.

Let's start mixing our values.

Squeeze out three inches of white paint on the upper-left corner of the palette. Next, place half the black paint that you have just mixed in the upper-right corner of your palette. Consider white the number one value, and black the number nine value. Your task now is to mix the seven steps of grays which lie between. Do all mixing on the lower half of the palette.

Take half of the black paint left in the mixing area. Add to it an equal amount of white paint. Mix together thoroughly, and the resulting gray color should be approximately a number five value.

By adding decreasing quantities of white to some of the number five value gray, you will produce values two, three and four. By adding increasing quantities of black to this number five gray, you will produce values six, seven and eight.

This is the simplest way to obtain nine values. The following way— which I use—is a more accurate way. You may prefer one, or you may want to try both methods.

Set up your number one value, white, and your number nine value, black. Now mix the number two value. Start with white and add a very small amount of black. Place this number two value at the top of the palette next to the white, leaving some space between them.

The important idea to keep in mind is: *If you are mixing for a light color, start with the lighter color of the mix. If you are trying for a dark color, start with the darker color of the mix.* It takes an almost microscopic amount of black to change white to a gray of a number two value. If you start with black, you will undoubtedly get the mixture too dark. A very small amount of white will destroy a good dark. This suggestion will apply to your later painting when you are working with many colors of different values.

It might be well now to mix the number eight value, after which you will set it up next to the number nine. Don't forget to start the mix with the black, the darkest value, adding the white to it. Continue with number three, then number seven. Follow these with numbers four and six. Finally, you arrive at number five, which is the halftone.

To test the accuracy of gradation, paint your nine values in a series, one below the other, on a small piece of canvas. Start at the top with a wide brush stroke (about four inches long) of the number one value—white. Clean your brush after each of the brush strokes. Beneath the white place a similar brush stroke of your number two value, so that it touches but does not blend. Continue with a brush stroke of each of the remaining values in their numerical order. If you enjoy excellence, you will prefer to do this exercise until you have a perfect gradation from values one through nine.

ASSIGNMENT 1

Use a 20 by 24 inch canvas board for this assignment. Draw two vertical lines on your canvas board, dividing it into approximately equal areas. To do this, use a brush which has been dipped into the thinner in which you have cleaned your brushes. This thin mixture of color is very good for sketching on canvas because it can be wiped off with a paint rag if you want to make a correction. It also dries quickly so you can paint over it almost immediately.

Paint the area on the left with white paint, value one. Paint the next area with black paint, value nine. Paint the third area with gray paint, value five. Where two areas come together, the paint should be touching but not blended.

On the white area, about four inches from the top, make a row of dots with your small brush (no. 6) dipped into the gray paint. About four inches below this draw a wavy line with the same color. Repeat the dots four inches below this line. Add another wavy line four inches from the bottom of the canvas.

Draw the same pattern on the black area in white paint. Draw the same pattern on the gray area with black paint.

This will give you an idea of how interesting different combinations of values can be in the same color.

ASSIGNMENT 2

For this assignment you will need a 20 by 24 inch canvas, and sections of newspapers that contain a number of ads or pictures in black and white.

At this point, if I were to ask you to paint a nonobjective picture, you might want to give up. It seems difficult for the beginner to originate abstract designs. There is a simple method of approach to this problem.

Your assignment is to paint a nonobjective picture in several values: black, white and grays. To find a pattern for your design you will choose pictures in several values from the newspaper sections. In order to avoid the reality of these pictures or ads, you will use them upside-down. Look for an area of related shapes in differing values: white, black and any values in grays. When you find an interesting area in these values, cut it out of the paper in a shape approximating the shape of your canvas.

Now with a small brush and very thin paint, sketch this design freely on your canvas. Do not measure—approximate the areas. As you draw the shapes, place the value numbers—for example, one, five or nine —in the center of each so that you will not have to refer to the clipping again. Paint your picture carefully with smooth edges between the values. If this is painted freely on the canvas, the resulting picture will be almost your own creation. Do not become dependent on this method of finding designs; it is meant merely to stimulate the imagination.

Information Briefs

COMPOSITION

Although this is a book about color, a short discussion of composition may help the beginner. There are no hard and fast rules for composition. One can only make suggestions which may or may not work for someone else. In fact there are lots of don'ts, but competent artists are constantly trying the don'ts and proving that they can be done.

Composition is the distribution and orderly arrangement of spaces and objects, each presented in its due proportion. It is not a haphazard gathering of miscellaneous objects in order to fill up space. Composition requires critical judgment as to space division, the placement of objects, their harmony of proportion, their relationships, light values and colors.

Our first consideration is space division. A painting which is divided exactly or seemingly halfway between the top and bottom of the canvas, or between left and right, is somewhat unpleasant because the observer constantly tries to compare the spaces. A more pleasing arrangement uses the space division of one-third and two-thirds. The divisions are both horizontal and vertical, and create four unequal areas.

Vertical lines or shapes and horizontal lines or shapes are stabilizing.

They keep the pattern of the picture from revolving. These lines and shapes are restful and reassuring. Horizontal lines represent the ground on which we walk. The houses that we live in have vertical walls and level floors.

Diagonal lines or areas, however small, attract the eye. If there are two or more diagonal lines or shapes, excitement is caused as the eye moves rapidly from one to the other. This quality in a painting is called "tension."

When there is a diagonal line or pattern in a painting, there should be an opposing diagonal thrust somewhere else in the painting. It need not be large, or at right angles, but the tension should be there.

If there are too many diagonal lines or shapes moving in one direction only, the picture appears to be tilted or unbalanced. Diagonal lines or areas which point toward the corner of the canvas tend to lead the observer out of the picture. This can be avoided by changing the direction of the diagonal slightly. Undulating lines or shapes, which suggest movement, are pleasing and decorative.

Though these are simple rules, they are the basics on which more complicated structures in painting are developed.

AND BABY BEAR

You may sometimes get the feeling that your painting is falling apart. The instructor urges you to "pull it together." But how? You find your picture composed of many small shapes that are alike in size and volume, causing a feeling of disorder or one of monotony.

One of my most revered teachers, Emil Bisttram, used psychology in his teaching. He claimed that we instinctively seek the family life pattern in any painting, whether realistic or nonobjective. He suggested that we think of the father, mother and child. By combining the small shapes, order comes to our painting—negative spaces as well as positive shapes are improved.

A fanciful way of remembering is to recall the Three Bears—papa bear, mama bear and baby bear. So in your picture paint a large shape, a medium-sized shape and a small shape, or an arrangement of small shapes. Who knows? There may have been more than one baby bear.

Lesson 2:
Primaries and Secondaries

Every time I teach this lesson I am reminded of the old saying, "A journey of a thousand miles starts with a single step." This lesson is the first step of a pleasant journey into color.

Before you begin mixing the paints for this lesson, take your pencil and draw a circle about six or eight inches in diameter. Divide the circle into thirds by placing a mark on the left for red, a mark at the top for yellow, and a mark at the right for blue. Next mark the secondary colors. Halfway between red and yellow place a mark for orange, halfway between yellow and blue place a mark for green, and halfway between blue and red place a mark for purple. Close your eyes and try to see these colors in your mind.

Although the spectrum colors appear in a horizontal band, it is helpful in our study of colors to think of them in a circular pattern. My reason for this is twofold: first, when the primary colors and the secondary colors are in a straight line, the beginning student fails to associate the secondary color, purple, with the primary color, red. It is

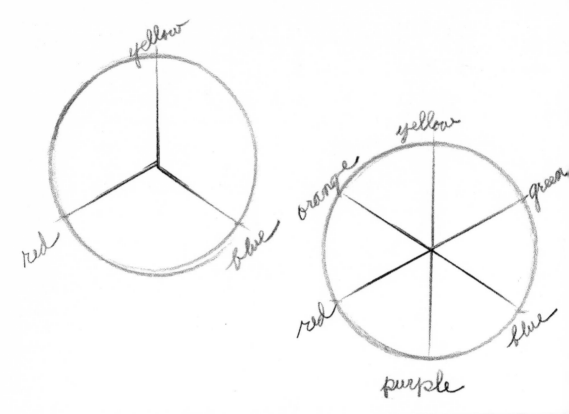

easy to understand that red and yellow make orange, and that yellow and blue make green, but purple, at the end of the line, seems to be unrelated to red which is at the beginning of that line. When the colors are placed in a circle, the student readily sees that purple lies between blue and red.

My second reason for the circle is to demonstrate a convenient way to locate the complementary colors. In a color wheel the complement of a color lies directly across the color wheel on a line drawn through the center of the circle. As an example, place a pencil dot in the center of your color wheel. Draw a line from the point marked red, through the center dot to the opposite side of the wheel. The line will connect with the mark termed green. Green is the complement of red; and, in reverse, red is the complement of green. Draw lines between yellow and purple, which are complementary to each other, and between blue and orange, also complementary to each other.

The pigment colors are placed along the upper part of the palette in a horizontal line in the order of the colors of the spectrum band, that is—R, O, Y, G, B, P.

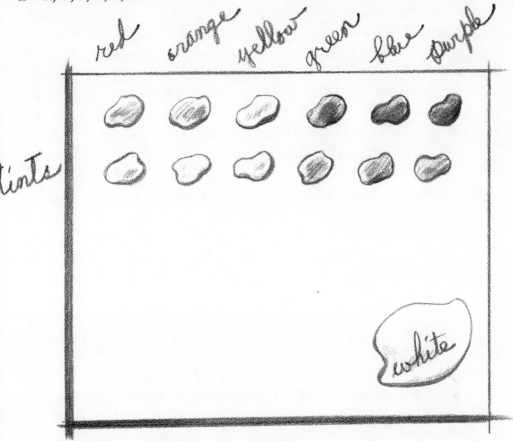

I will be very specific about the arrangement of colors on the palette. A careless arrangement makes it necessary to search for the color wanted. It is similar to the "hunt and peck" system of typing. It is a waste of time. Since reds, yellows and blues will always be used, the painter should be able to reach for them almost without looking.

Imagine that your palette is divided along the top edge into six equal spaces. Spaces one, three and five are to be occupied by the primary colors. Spaces two, four and six will be used for the secondary colors after you have mixed them.

Again in this lesson we are using cadmium red light, cadmium yellow light, ultramarine blue, and titanium or zinc white. We learned from the spectrum, and from the rainbow, that the primary colors merge with one another to form what we know as the secondary colors. Red merges with yellow to form orange; yellow merges with blue to form green; and blue merges with red to form purple.

Squeeze about two inches of cadmium red light onto your palette in the upper-left corner—not too near the edges. This is always the place for the red, or reds. Next squeeze out six inches of yellow and place it in the third space. Yellow will always be in this space. Finally squeeze out three inches of blue and place it in the fifth space. This will always be the location for any blue color, or colors.

The beginning student may assume that all pigments of colors are of equal strength, because the spectrum colors are of equal brilliance. These are light rays. The pigments as they come from the tubes differ greatly in intensity—in strength. Red is a very strong pigment, yellow is a weak pigment, and blue is a strong pigment, but not as strong as red.

To produce the color orange, take about one third of the yellow with your palette knife and place it in the mixing area of the palette. Wipe your knife, and take a very small amount of red. Mix it with the yellow, lifting it with the knife and spreading it somewhat. Don't pat it—mix it. If it is not what you consider a good orange, add some more red. If it is already too red, add more yellow. Try to make a precise color of orange. Place the color you have mixed between the red and yellow at the top of your palette. Wipe your knife carefully and clean the orange paint from the mixing area.

To produce the color green, take two inches of yellow and place it in the mixing area. Add a small amount of blue, and mix these together. You should come up with a lively green, neither a yellow-green nor a blue-green. Place this green between the yellow and blue at the top of your palette. Wipe your knife and clean the mixing area again.

To mix purple, place about one inch of blue in the mixing area. With your knife add about half as much red and mix well. You will find that you have a color which, like black, is below the threshold of sight. In order to determine the exact color, mix a small amount of purple with a small amount of white. It should produce a light value of violet (purple). Most students insist that it is brown, but on your canvas it will appear a true purple in relation to all the other colors produced by this triad of red, yellow and blue.

If the violet seems too red, add a bit more blue to the dark mass of purple. If it seems too blue add a bit more red. Place the purple at the top of the palette halfway between the blue and the right edge of the palette.

Now you have the primaries and secondaries across the top of the palette in a horizontal line—red, orange, yellow, green, blue and purple.

Squeeze out about three inches of white paint and place it at center-right in the mixing area of the palette. This location can be changed at your convenience.

Let us now examine the values of the colors that we have just mixed, with reference to the nine values in black and white of our first lesson.

The lightest color on the palette is yellow. It is such a light value, let us consider it as the number one value. Orange, which contains so much yellow, is the next—it should be about a value three. Cadmium red light is usually considered a value five. The color green should also be about a value five; however, it is a cool color and may appear to be darker than the red. We have already learned that certain colors are cool or receding because of the way in which reflected light rays affect our eyes. Just as the reflected light rays cause our eyes to see the reds and yellows as if they are nearer than they actually are, they also cause us to see blues or greens as if they were farther away.

Blue is also a cool color of great intensity. In value it is considered a number nine because it is so near the threshold of sight. Purple is also a number nine value. It is not as cool as blue because it contains some red, which causes it to be slightly warmer than the pure blue.

There are no set rules for value estimates. Your own sensitivity is what you must rely on. We number the values only as a means of communication. The amount of light in a color in your paintings is as important as the color itself.

In a painting you must also be aware that there are values in areas.

There are light areas that may contain several colors, and dark areas which may contain more than one color. So we may speak of an area as having a number three or four value, for example.

By mixing white with any color, we produce what is known as a tint of that color. Any color of a nine value—ultramarine blue for instance—has the same number of tints as the color black of the first lesson. These tints would be a gradation of blues from a very light blue to a blue of a dark value. These are all "tints" of blue. Cadmium red light—which is approximately a number five value—cannot have any tints darker than the original red. However, due to the intensity of the pigment, we can produce magnificent and brilliant tints from this pigment. Yellow, which seems so very light, can be made still lighter by the addition of white.

Many more tints may be made from these colors, but for the purpose of communication, we designate tints in these lessons by their approximate numbers in the value scale of one to nine.

Mix two tints of each of the six colors on your palette: one a very light tint, a value three; and one a darker tint—a value four for the light colors, and a value six for the dark colors.

You will observe that although the light tints of these six colors are all the same value (three), some colors will seem more brilliant than others. This is because the colors containing red and yellow are warm advancing colors. The light tints which contain blue seem cool and receding.

This lesson sets up the procedure that you will follow as long as you study color. Each time in the future, when you choose your own triad, you will place the red, the yellow and the blue in exactly the same places that you used for the primary colors of this lesson. You will then immediately mix the secondary colors which your new triad will produce.

ASSIGNMENT

For this assignment, use a 20 by 24 inch canvas vertically. Divide the canvas into six vertical stripes, each approximately three inches in width. Paint the first vertical stripe orange, and the second stripe yellow.

Paint the third stripe a tint of purple, in about a five value. Be sure that it is not too dark. For the fourth stripe use red from the tube. Paint the fifth stripe a tint of blue in a five value. For the last stripe use a tint of green in a four value. To finish the painting add very thin lines of brilliant tints of the six colors. Paint lines between the stripes, and add more lines on the stripes, such as a yellow-green tint on the red stripe, or a tint of orange on the purple stripe.

This is your first acquaintance with color and color values. Don't be afraid to try unusual combinations with the narrow colored lines. Find exciting combinations.

Lesson 3:
Color Intervals

In the previous lesson you painted with six colors and their tints, a somewhat limited range of colors. In this lesson we will double the number of colors.

As in the last lesson, draw a circle about six or eight inches in diameter. Place marks for the primary colors, designating them by their initials, R, Y, B—red, yellow and blue. Next mark the secondary colors orange, green and purple, also designating them by their initials. Close your eyes and try to see these colors in your mind.

In order to develop a greater selection, we will produce intervals of colors between the primaries and secondaries, as shown in the diagram.

Place a pencil mark between red and orange and designate it red-orange (R-O). Place a mark between orange and yellow, naming it orange-yellow (O-Y). Between the extremes of the colors red and yellow there can be no color other than orange—it may be a red-orange or a yellow-orange, but it will always be the color orange.

42

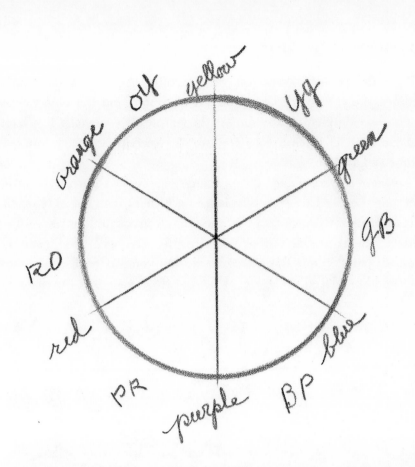

Next place a mark between yellow and green, calling it yellow-green (Y-G). Mark between green and blue, and call it green-blue. (G-B). Between the extreme colors of yellow and blue there can be no color other than green. It may be a yellow-green or a blue-green, but it is always a green.

Place a mark between blue and purple naming it blue-purple (B-P). Place a mark between purple and red, naming it purple-red (P-R). Between the extreme colors of blue and red there can be no color other than purple. It may be a blue-purple or a red-purple, but it is always a purple.

Try to visualize what these new colors will look like. These are color intervals. These twelve intervals of color are a part of your color alphabet.

Now we are ready to actually mix the color intervals, using cadmium red light, cadmium yellow light, ultramarine blue and zinc white or titanium white.

Place the primary colors on your palette: the red in the upper-left corner, the yellow a little to the left of center, and the blue toward the right, leaving plenty of space for the purple. If you make it a habit to put the triad in place before you mix the secondary colors, you will save time and avoid confusion.

Now mix the secondary colors orange, green and purple. In order to ascertain the exact color of purple, put a little of it to one side on the palette and mix it with white. Place the orange, green and purple in their respective places at the top of your palette. You will need generous amounts of paint to mix these secondaries. As you mix each color interval, it should be placed at the top of the palette as shown in the diagram.

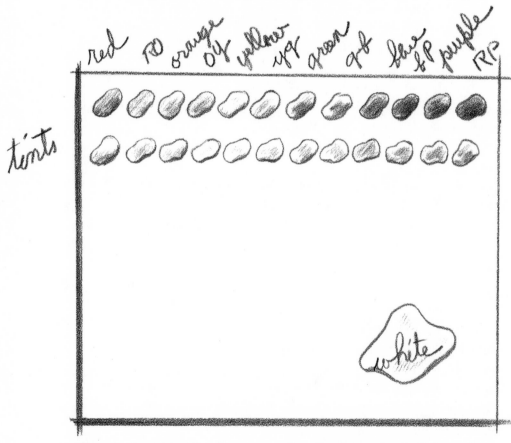

To mix the interval red-orange, take about one-third of the orange and place it in the mixing area. Add a very small amount of red, and judge whether this new color is halfway between red and orange.

To mix orange-yellow, take some yellow and place it in the mixing area. Remember to start with the lighter color in this mix. Add a very small amount of orange. Orange-yellow should be quite yellowish. Place this color at the top of the palette between orange and yellow. Clean the mixing area.

To produce yellow-green place some yellow in the mixing area and add a very small amount of green. Yellow-green should also be quite yellowish.

To produce blue-green start with green in the mixing area. Add a small amount of blue. This color will be very dark, so move some of it to one side of the palette with your knife and add a small amount of white to be sure that it is blue-green. Place this color at the top of the palette between green and blue. Again clean the mixing area.

To mix blue-purple place some purple in the mixing area and add some blue. Test to make sure of the color.

Finally, to produce red-purple, place some purple in the mixing area and add a little red. The red-purple can be quite reddish. Be sure to test a sample of it.

When you are trying to decide whether you have mixed the correct color for the interval—yellow-green, for instance—ask yourself, "If I came upon this color suddenly, would I think yellow-green, or would I think green?" Do this for all your intervals.

Draw lines on your color wheel between the complementary colors: red and green, yellow and purple, blue and orange. Now draw lines between the color intervals and their complementaries, that is, red-orange and blue-green, and so on.

The next step is to mix a tint of each of these colors in about a number four value. Be sure that the tints of the cool dark colors are light enough. For some reason students often feel that the tints of the dark colors should be relatively darker than the tints of the light colors. As an example, a tint of blue-green in this problem should be no darker than the tint of red-orange. Tints of the darker colors require more white paint than tints of the light colors.

ASSIGNMENT 1

This will be an exercise in which you investigate color perspective. Imagine that you are standing in a field of flowers so vast that they reach the horizon. I have seen such fields of wild flowers in California. Near Lompoc, there are wide fields of cultivated flowers grown especially for seed companies.

Today you will use all the colors you have on your palette, because in this painting we are going to suggest such a field of flowers. Your problem is to remember which colors give the effect of distance, and which come forward.

Use a 20 by 24 inch canvas horizontally. With your brush draw a horizon line about one-third down from the top. Do not measure, estimate it. Paint the sky a very light blue. Paint low hills just above the horizon line.

The flowers are to be merely brush strokes. Starting at the left below the horizon line, make short vertical brush strokes about two inches in height, using cool colors in a very light value to give the effect of distance. When you see flowers at a distance they have no form—they are mere spots of color.

In the far distance, just below the horizon, the values may be very light tints of the purples and blues. A light tint of red-purple may give the effect of distant pink flowers. The values become slightly darker and more brilliant as they approach the foreground.

There should be about five rows of brush strokes from the horizon to the foreground, each one wider and taller than the one above. The rows may be slightly diagonal and irregular, but the brush strokes should always be vertical and touching at the sides, but not blending.

Continue the second row of strokes from left to right as you proceed down the canvas, overlapping each row. With each row the brush strokes become taller and wider until in the foreground they may be four inches tall. They are to be brush strokes—no actual flowers.

Throughout the picture you may use accents of green in different values, dark brilliant greens in the foreground and a very light blue-green in the distance. In the foreground very brilliant tints of pink, orange and yellow will strengthen the effect of a field stretching far into the distance.

Be very free with this painting and have fun.

ASSIGNMENT 2

In the previous assignment you studied the effect of warm and cool colors in small shapes, that is, brush strokes. In this assignment you are to study the effect of large areas of color in relation to each other, and in relation to the picture as a whole.

Paint a nonobjective picture in geometric shapes—rectangles, squares, circles and parts of circles. Use no more than twenty shapes, some large and some medium size. Do not use all the colors on your palette, be selective. Remember that white is a color also.

When you have made a drawing with your brush and decided what your colors will be, do not outline the shapes and "fill in" as a child does with a coloring book. Start with brush strokes of paint in the middle of each shape and work toward the edges. Where two colors meet, the colors should touch but not blend. However, do not try for the professional hard-edge effect. Your problem is the use of areas of pure colors, and areas of tints of pure colors, in various values to produce a total harmonious effect.

Information Briefs

YOUR PAINTING STYLE

Reading a book does not make you an artist. No matter how well you understand what the book teaches, you will be unable to express yourself in painting until you put color on canvas. The directions suggested here will take you past that first moment when, with a brushful of paint in hand, you face a large white canvas. A discussion of painting styles may help you find a direction.

There have been new and perhaps strange styles of painting since the time nearly a century ago when artists chose to abandon the traditional rules and disciplines of realistic painting. They adopted freer and more personal forms to express themselves. These styles have gained acceptance as valid forms of painting. In fact, there was a period in which drawing was dismissed entirely.

Students want to know the meaning of the terms abstract, semiabstract, nonobjective, nonfigurative and even nonreferential. These divisions tend to overlap and become confused. To define these styles is difficult because opinions differ as to their meanings.

As a teacher, I have given my interpretation by dividing the styles of painting into three fairly well-defined groups: representational or realistic painting, abstract painting and nonobjective painting.

In representational art, the subject matter is presented in a more or less photographic manner. This style of painting is sometimes called realistic, or realism. Realistic painting is three dimensional—forms have height, width and depth (perspective).

Abstract art is sometimes defined as that which does not recall reality, even of an accidental kind. I suppose some artists can accept that definition, but I find too many exceptions to it. Isn't the little stick figure a child makes with toothpicks an abstraction? Yet it certainly recalls reality. The paintings of Braque are abstractions, but they recall musical instruments, tables and bowls of fruit, stated in slightly distorted shapes and unusual space arrangements. Some of Picasso's paintings are certainly abstract, although they recall reality.

I define "abstract" art as that in which the subject matter is presented through unusual space arrangements and interpretive elements. Simplified or distorted images are used as symbols to suggest but not define the artist's intense inner feelings. Abstract painting may be either two-dimensional, having only height and width, or three-dimensional.

Nonobjective art has no recognizable images—the color, composition and textures are the subject matter. Color is used as a powerful means of expressing emotions and feelings from the tragic to the serene. This style expresses the feeling of a third dimension, or depth, by means of the juxtaposition of warm and cool color, as well as by the overlapping of shapes; but the shapes and areas of space are generally two-dimensional. Nonobjective is the most descriptive term to describe the third style of painting.

I recommend the nonobjective style of painting for the study of color. The student can concentrate on the relationship of colors, the vibration of colors, and the effects of warm and cool color without the distraction of developing recognizable forms.

SIMPLE LANDSCAPE VALUES

The landscape seems to be a favorite subject for painters. They paint an infinite variety of arrangements of sky, hills, trees, earth and sea.

The beginning landscape painter will be helped by analyzing the dark and light value patterns before putting paint on canvas. We are often inclined to paint the leaves on the trees before establishing this simple dark-light pattern of our landscapes.

The sky is the source of light. Around midday it is the lightest value. The light falls on the ground, which reflects it directly. The ground becomes the second lightest value in a painting. Hills slope diagonally away from the ground; for this reason they reflect less light. This area is darker than the previous two areas. Trees and bushes are darkest at this time of day because they are vertical shapes. The light strikes only the tops of them.

At midday the values in the scale of nine (from brightest light to darkest dark) might be: sky, number two value; earth, number four value; hills, number six value; trees, number eight.

The values change with the time of day. In the late afternoon the direct light of the sun falls on the sides of the trees and they become one of the lighter values. There are stormy days when the sky is the darkest value. For these changes the painter must adjust the other values in the painting accordingly. For the overall pattern four simple values should be enough.

In each individual pattern there are variations in the values—small changes of light, dark and halftones in the trees for instance, and on the ground.

Clouds in the sky, if painted with strong contrast of light and dark, tend to destroy the overall value pattern of a painting. These details often cause the clouds to float forward and appear in the middle distance. Consider sky and clouds as one value unit in a painting.

WASHES

A wash is a very thin layer of paint diluted with thinner or turpentine, usually brushed on the canvas at the start of a painting to establish the large areas of dark and light or warm and cool.

There are flat washes and washes with gradation. A flat wash is color or a number of colors of the same value applied over a determined area.

Gradation means a gradual change in values from light to dark or dark to light. A graded wash might be a wash of light green gradually becoming a darker green. It might also be a wash of a dark pink gradually becoming a very light pink. The gradation may go from top to bottom, or from side to side.

Lesson 4:
Graying the Colors

Draw the color wheel six or eight inches in diameter. Mark the places for the primary colors and designate them R, Y, B, visualizing each color as you write the name. Then mark the secondary colors, designating them O, G, P, keeping these colors in your mind also.

Set up the pigment colors, red, yellow and blue, at the top of the palette in their respective places. Mix the secondary colors, orange, green and purple, and place them between the primary colors at the top of the palette.

Mix a tint of each of the colors in about a number four value, placing each tint below the original pure color. Make sure that the cool tints are not darker in value than the warm tints—with the exception of the yellow, which is always a very light value.

Of all the lessons in this book, this one is the most important. It is somewhat difficult, but you will be repaid for every moment spent on it. It would benefit you to do this lesson two or three times before going on to the next lesson.

In our first lesson we learned that white contains all color and reflects all color. Therefore, red plus yellow plus blue equals white. Since black absorbs all color, it follows that red plus yellow plus blue also equals black.

The colors on your palette are beautiful, but they are somewhat obvious—some are even harsh. We can make colors more pleasingly subtle or subdued by "graying" them.

In order to "gray" the red color, we must add the other two colors needed to make up black—that is, yellow and blue. A mixture of yellow and blue is green. Therefore, to gray the red, we add a small amount of green.

To gray the color yellow we must add blue and red. Since a mixture of blue and red is purple, the color yellow is grayed by the addition of a small amount of purple.

To gray the color blue, we must add a small amount of red and yellow. Since the mixture of red and yellow is orange, we use orange to gray the color blue.

To gray the secondary colors, the same process is followed. Since orange already contains two colors (red and yellow), we gray the orange by adding a small amount of blue.

To gray the green, which already contains two colors (yellow and blue), we add a small amount of red.

To gray the purple, which contains red and blue, we add a small amount of yellow.

Translated into a simple rule: *Any color may be grayed by adding a small amount of its complementary color.*

I hope that you have already memorized the complementary colors: red and green, yellow and purple, blue and orange. Look at your color wheel and observe again that the complementary colors are directly across from each other on a line through the center of the color wheel.

We now proceed to gray the colors. You have on your palette the pure colors—the primaries and secondaries and a tint of each of them.

Take some of the tint of red (pink) and place it in the mixing area. Add a small amount of the tint of green and mix well. If the mixture loses its pinkish quality, you have added too much green. Put some more of the pink back into it. The result should be a lovely grayed pink.

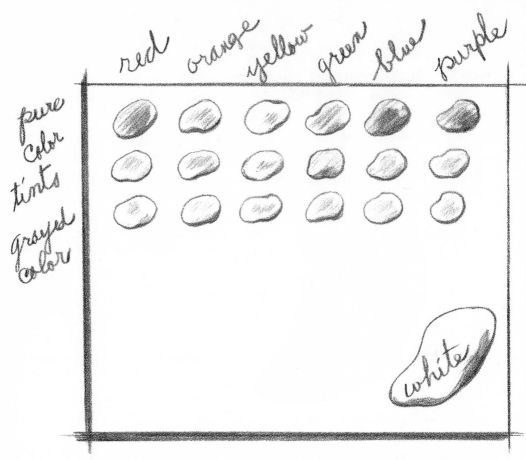

Do the same with a tint of orange—place some in the mixing area and add a small amount of blue. This must be done carefully. If the value of the blue tint is the least bit too dark, the grayed orange will appear green. The grayed orange must appear to be a warm color.

Yellow color is the most difficult to gray. It is a color which is light in value, and as a pigment color, is very weak. Since purple is composed of two very strong pigment colors, it is necessary to add white to the purple tint until it becomes a very light (violet) purple. Otherwise, the purple will "eat up" the yellow.

Now gray the tints of the cool colors, green, blue and purple, by placing each tint in the mixing area and graying it with its complementary. Remember that each of these should retain its own color identity.

The reason we use the tints of colors for the graying is because we need to see each color clearly as the graying takes place. Your next graying will be done with the pure colors, and you will find it difficult to observe the change in these dark colors because they are so near the threshold of sight.

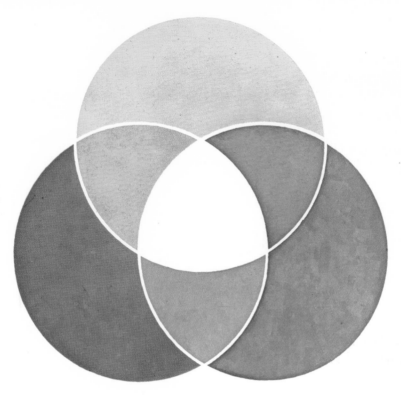

COLOR CHART: PRIMARY AND SECONDARY COLORS
Catherine Hagen • *Oil on Canvas*

COLOR CHART: PRIMARIES, SECONDARIES AND INTERVALS
Catherine Hagen • *Oil on Canvas*

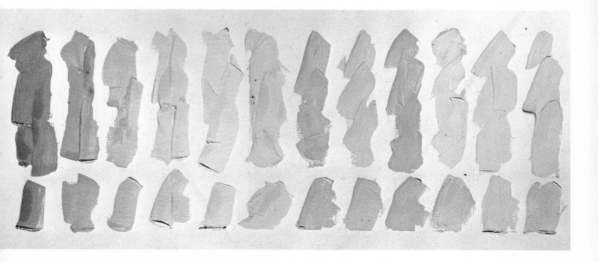

COLOR CHART: VALUES—TRIANGLES
Catherine Hagen • *Oil on Canvas*

COLOR CHART: ANALOGOUS COLOR—RED
Catherine Hagen • *Oil on Canvas*

BICYCLES IN THE RAIN *Catherine Hagen* • *Oil on Canvas*

COLOR CHART: ANALOGOUS COLOR—YELLOW
Catherine Hagen • *Oil on Canvas*

COLOR CHART: ANALOGOUS COLOR—BLUE
Catherine Hagen • *Oil on Canvas*

ACCENT ON RED *Catherine Hagen* • *Watercolor*

CHRYSANTHEMUMS AND STILL LIFE   *Catherine Hagen*   •   *Oil on Canvas*

LANDSCAPE IN PURE COLOR   *Catherine Hagen*   •   *Oil on Canvas*

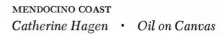

MENDOCINO COAST
Catherine Hagen • *Oil on Canvas*

SALT RIVER VALLEY
Catherine Hagen • *Oil on Canvas*

IRIS FOLIAGE PATTERN
Catherine Hagen • *Acrylic on Canvas*

ORIENTAL POPPIES
Catherine Hagen • *Watercolor*

SUMMER FLORAL
Catherine Hagen • *Watercolor*

GUATEMALA SUN SERIES
Eleanor Elsocht • *Acrylic on Canvas*

BRIONES HILLS

Avis DeMonte • *Oil on Canvas*

LINDSEY CREEK PARK

Robert Elsocht • *Oil on Canvas*

MODOC
Marjorie Cathcart • Acrylic on Canvas

UPPER KLAMATH
Robert Elsocht • Oil on Canvas

FLAGS OF SPRING
Flora North • Acrylic

Take some of the pure red color and place it in the mixing area. Add a small amount of its complementary and mix well. It will appear a dark brick red. Repeat the process with the other pure colors, graying each with its pure color complementary. Now you have on your palette twenty-four variations of the spectrum colors: the top row of six are the primary and secondary pure colors. The next row of six are the tints of the pure colors; the third row of six colors are the grayed tints of the colors; the fourth row of six are the pure colors grayed by their pure color complementaries.

You have learned the method of graying each color with its exact complementary. In later lessons you will find variations of this system, but the principle remains the same for developing subtle and unusual colors.

ASSIGNMENT 1

Use a 20 by 24 inch canvas board horizontally. This assignment is not a painting, but a diagram showing the use of three values in each color to produce the effect of form. (A shape is two-dimensional, having height and width. A form is three-dimensional, with height, width and depth.)

With a brush dipped in very thin paint, draw six fairly large, simple shapes: three cylinders and three circles. Two of the cylinders should be vertical, one tall and one short. The third cylinder should be rather short and lying horizontally. These figures represent fruit for a still-life painting in our next assignment.

Divide the vertical cylinders into three fairly equal vertical areas. Divide the horizontal cylinder into three horizontal areas. Divide the circles into three vertical areas, following the shape of the circle, thus making some crescent-shaped areas.

In the first circle, paint the left area a tint of red, the middle area a pure red, and the third area pure red grayed by its complementary. Paint the next circle from left to right a tint of orange, the middle area pure orange, and the third area pure orange grayed with its complementary. Paint the horizontal cylinder a tint of yellow on the top area, the second area pure yellow, and the third or bottom area a pure yellow grayed with its complementary color. Paint the short vertical cylinder from left to right a tint of green in a four value, the second area a tint of blue-green in a five value, and the third area the same tint of blue-green grayed with its complementary. Paint the tall cylinder from left to right, a tint of blue in a three value, the second area a tint of blue in a five value, and the third area the same tint of blue grayed with its complementary.

Paint the third circle from left to right, a very light tint of red-purple, the second area a tint of purple in a five value, and the third area, the same tint of purple grayed with its complementary.

This is a very mechanical demonstration of the development of form.

ASSIGNMENT 2

Use a 20 by 24 inch canvas horizontally. Your subject matter will be a dark red apple, an orange, a lemon, a green pepper, a blue vase and an eggplant or a red cabbage. With a brush dipped in thin paint make a still-life sketch, arranging the fruit in a pleasing manner. Make changes in the values to approximate the colors and values of the fruits.

If fruit is not available, use cups, bowls or other objects as substitutes. You may paint a white cloth on the table, but it should be painted with very light tints of colors which may be caused by reflections and shadows. The wall in the background may be painted a color of your choice in whatever value you prefer.

Information Briefs

SHADOWS AND REFLECTIONS

Outdoors, shadows are cool, highlights are warm. A shadow is a dark shape on the ground or on a surface. It is caused by a body intercepting light rays. Even without the definition we all know a shadow when we see one, so let's go on from there.

A shadow may fall in any direction depending on the source of light. The long shadows of early morning grow shorter toward noon, when they almost disappear. They fall in the opposite direction and become longer as the sun moves toward the western horizon. Your paintings may indicate the time of day by the shape and direction of shadows.

A square building does not necessarily cast a square shadow. The shape of the shadow depends not only on the shape of the object casting the shadow, but also on the shape of the surface on which it falls. From my window in the morning the shadow of our flat-roofed house falls in a sharp diagonal across the side of the garage and horizontally across the walk. It then rises in round shapes across some bushes and finally becomes a weird shape on a big old plum tree.

A shadow has no color of its own. In a realistic painting it must have some of the color of the object on which it falls. Let us say that a large tree casts a shadow across a patch of green grass, a sidewalk of gray concrete, and a patch of bright yellow flowers. The grass in the shadow is still green, although a darker grayed green; the sidewalk in shadow is still gray, although a darker gray; the yellow flowers are still yellow, although they are a darker grayed yellow.

A large shadow is lighter at the center than at the edges. This fact calls to mind the rule: when a dark area and a light area come together, the dark seems darker and the light seems lighter. Where the dark edge of the tree shadow meets the sunlit green of the grass, the shadow should be painted slightly darker, and the sunlit grass should be painted slightly lighter.

Indoors, when the source of light is a light bulb, shadows are cool because the light is yellow and has the same effect as sunlight. Indoors in natural light, shadows are warm and highlights are cool.

The color of shadows indoors follows the same rule: the color of the shadow is still the color of the object or surface on which it falls, although it will be a bit darker and more grayed. The shadow on a brown table is still brown, the shadow on a red cloth is still red, but both colors are a bit darker and grayed.

When a colorful object like an orange casts a shadow on a light surface, the shadow may contain the reflected color of the orange. In still-life painting the play of shadows and reflected colors is a fascinating challenge.

Reflections, unlike shadows, are not controlled by the source of light. The reflection falls in one direction only—toward the observer. Place some brightly colored objects, perhaps an orange, an apple and a lemon, on a shiny dark table. Their reflections fall toward you. Walk around the table and observe that the reflection has followed you. It is always between the object casting it and the observer.

This is also true outdoors near the water. When I look directly across the harbor, the reflections of the small buildings and the boats with their tall masts fall straight toward me. They are at right angles to the shoreline. Farther down along the same shore, the reflections of other tall masts fall diagonally across the water almost to my feet.

A NONOBJECTIVE PAINTING

Artists in all periods painted their observations and reactions to the times in which they lived. We live in a space age. The world has never experienced the events that are occurring today. In this painting you will try to express the adventure, the uncertainty and the excitement of our time by means of color, abstract shapes and textures.

No instructor can teach you how to paint an abstract or nonobjective painting. You can only be urged to make the attempt and the instructor can only offer a few mechanical suggestions to pave the way. Do not refer to a picture or diagram, and do not make a sketch on your canvas. Let this be your own spontaneous creation with color.

Use a large canvas more square than rectangular, and at least 24 by 28 inches or 28 by 32 inches. A large brush will be needed.

You should read this list of suggestions, then put the book away and forget everything but your color and your canvas.

Stand well back from the easel and hold your brush toward the end of the handle. Don't be afraid of this great white canvas, commit yourself. Put a splash of color on it. Paint freely and forget about neatness. Do not draw lines to outline the color shapes. Exclude from your mind all images of people or things. Be aware that a recognizable image is not necessary to a painting. Your composition itself, the colors, shapes and textures will be your subject matter. Think of areas, using rich colors, tints of colors and grayed colors. Remember that white is also a color. The colors should flow together freely with some hard edges, some blended edges. Don't scrub with your brush—paint with it. Try brush strokes of different lengths and directions. Turn the canvas upside down or sideways and paint on it that way for a while. Do not allow it to become a landscape. Get the feeling of motion or rhythm. Do not allow small exciting brilliant shapes to destroy the importance of the overall dark and light pattern of the large shapes.

You will find that your sense of proportion and balance will tell you where to add a color, where to change a shape. And when you have finished, you will be surprised at your sense of freedom and fine accomplishment.

Lesson 5:
A Low-Key Triad

There are keys in color just as there are keys in music. A key in music is defined as a system of related notes based on a keynote, and forming a given scale.

So far we have been painting in one key only, which we describe as the primary key—cadmium red light, cadmium yellow light and ultramarine blue. This is the Common Triad. If we were to change the red in this triad, the orange and purple would be entirely different. In other words, we would be painting in a different key. In this lesson we will develop a low-key triad.

In previous lessons we learned the basic rules by which we develop many colors from a given triad. In this lesson we will become aware of the remarkable versatility of the three primary colors. With them we will produce a low-key red, a low-key yellow and a low-key blue.

The method of converting the primary triad into another key is as follows: the three members of any triad are considered as and stand

equivalent for the three primary colors of the Common Triad. It may seem
clearer if I say that the new low-key red, yellow and blue will substitute
for the primary red, yellow and blue. Yet each of these new colors has
an identity of its own as soon as it is mixed. The painting which you will
produce from these colors will have a distinct quality that identifies it
as having been made from a low-key triad.

Before you start to mix the new colors, do not place the primary
colors at the top of the palette as you did in the previous lessons. This
space is reserved for the new low-key triad. We will use the primary
colors only in the mixing area.

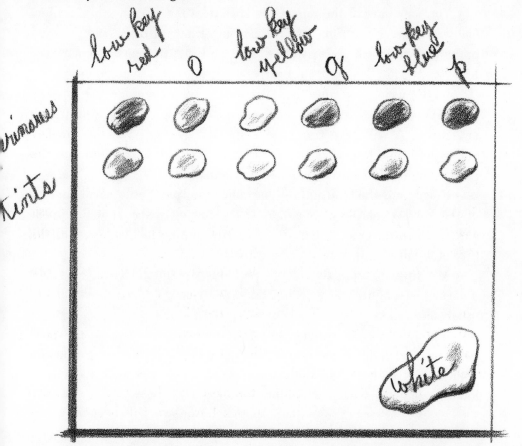

On your palette place an inch or so of cadmium red light, and
gray it with a dark green until it becomes a dark brick red. It should be
slightly toward brown rather than toward purple. Place it at the top of

your palette where you always keep red. Clean the mixing area. Next take three inches of cadmium yellow light and gray it with a tint of purple until it is a muddy yellow. Place this muddy yellow at the top of the palette where the yellow usually goes. Clean the mixing area.

Squeeze out about two inches of ultramarine blue in the mixing space and gray it with orange. It is rather difficult to gray the dark ultramarine blue with a mixed orange. A better way to produce a low-key blue is by the addition of the red and yellow separately. The blue should be a blackish blue. Place it at the top of the palette in the blue space, and clean the mixing area.

You now have at the top of your palette a red, a yellow and a blue. Consider these your primaries for this triad. If any of these colors is used up before you finish your painting, stop and mix the missing color. Try to match the low-key colors as nearly as possible before you go on.

In the usual way, mix the secondary colors. Combine the low-key red and the low-key yellow to make orange. Be prepared to find a strange orange but it will be a true orange in this low key. Mix the low-key yellow and blue to get the secondary green. It will look muddy on the palette, but on the canvas it will be very handsome.

Finally mix the blue and red to produce purple. Test a small amount of the low-key purple at one side of the mixing space. It may appear almost a neutral gray, but it will be a true purple in this key, and the tints of it will appear violet on your canvas.

Mix tints of these six colors—perhaps two tints of each, one dark and one very light. You will find that you have produced new and unusual colors.

It might be well to note here that you must avoid using the pure cadmium red light, cadmium yellow light or the ultramarine blue on your canvas with the low-key colors. The pure colors will make your low-key colors seem drab and uninteresting.

ASSIGNMENT 1

Use a 20 by 24 inch canvas board. Make a design or nonobjective study in geometric shapes in order to become acquainted with these colors and their tints. Use a hard-edge style, but leave a narrow space of the white canvas between all of the shapes. This white line is sometimes very pleasing.

ASSIGNMENT 2

These colors suggest to me the outdoors—great rocks or canyons or deserts under a dark sky.

They could be the colors of a day in late autumn. Make your own decision as to what these colors mean to you. Paint a picture on a large canvas 24 by 28 inches or larger, using a large brush.

EXPANDING
THE PRIMARIES

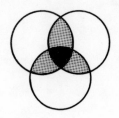

Lesson 6:
A New Triad

In previous lessons I have opened a door to a garden of new and imaginative colors, made from only three pigment colors. Once you have made these colors and are able to reproduce them at will, you are ready to learn how the basic principles of the primary colors can be applied to the array of tube colors available.

I will restate that a triad may be formed by the selection of any red, any yellow and any blue. In this lesson you will use a color called "alizarin crimson," a dark purplish red.

Make a pencil color wheel and in place of the word "red" write "alizarin crimson." This color has not usurped the place of cadmium red light. The new color will be set up as a basic part of the new triad. Seeing it on the color wheel will enable you to visualize it in this new triad. Mark the yellow and blue as usual.

In this new adventure into color we will make one change only, substituting alizarin crimson for cadmium red light. The yellow in the

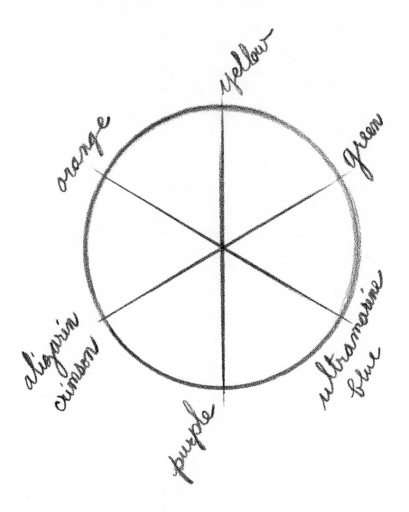

triad will remain cadmium yellow light and the blue, ultramarine blue. You will see how this one new color will influence most of the other colors, tints and grayed colors.

At the top of your palette place some alizarin crimson in the space always occupied by red. This will be your only red. Place yellow and blue in their usual spaces. Mix the secondary colors of this triad by combining alizarin crimson and yellow in the mixing area to produce orange. You will find that in spite of the very dark red, your orange color will be quite brilliant. Set it up at the top of the palette in the space for orange. Clean the mixing area.

Mix cadmium yellow light and ultramarine blue to form a bright green. Place it as usual at the top of the palette. Clean the mixing area.

In the mixing area place equal amounts of alizarin crimson and ultramarine blue to produce the purple of this triad. Test the purple by mixing a small sample of it with white at the right side of your palette. You will be pleased to find that you have a purple that "looks" like a purple. It should be a royal purple. Place it at the top of your palette in the purple space.

Make tints of the six colors in about a four value. You will note that a tint of alizarin crimson is a very cool pink.

Gray the six tints with tints of their complementary colors. You may want to gray some of the pure colors.

If you wish to use the interval colors—RO, OY, YG, GB, BP and PR—you may mix them as you work.

More than half of the colors on your palette are entirely new, as your next picture will reflect.

ASSIGNMENT

Paint a still-life painting using a variety of fruits and vegetables as you did in Lesson Four, with vase, drapery and background of your own

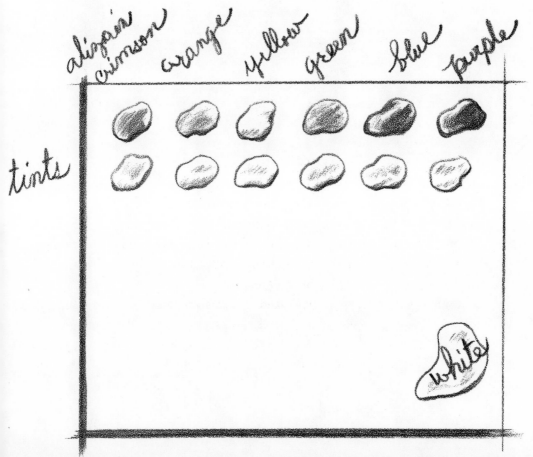

choosing. Many students say, "But I don't like still-life painting," or, "What will I do with a still-life painting?" I counter this with, "Throw it away, or burn it after it is finished. But paint it!" Still-life painting can teach you all the principles of painting—color, composition, values, form, perspective, rhythm and texture. I think it was Cezanne who said, "After you have finished such a painting, you can always eat it."

Lesson 7:
More New Triads

This lesson describes two new triads in the extremes of color—one very low-key and the other a very high-key. These color patterns should not be painted at the same time, as each has a special mood for which the subject matter should be chosen with care and sensitivity.

LOW-KEY TRIAD

Earth colors make a handsome low-key color pattern. We will use burnt sienna as the red and yellow ochre as the yellow—the same colors as those used by primitive artists. For blue, charcoal or soot was used; we will use black tube paint, which in reality is a very dark blue.

Some students find that the secondary colors produced by black, that is, green and purple, are too grayed. Therefore, I suggest that a small amount of ultramarine blue be added to the black tube paint in the mixing area before setting it up at the top of the palette.

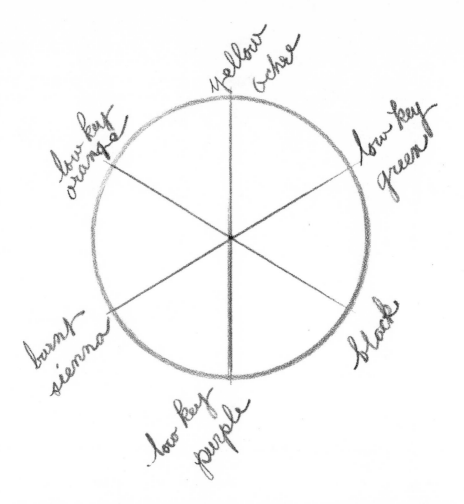

Make sure there is no cadmium red light, cadmium yellow light or pure ultramarine blue on your palette while you are painting with this low-key triad—they would make the earth colors seem drab and colorless.

Place some burnt sienna in the red space at the top of your palette; this will be your only red. Place a generous amount of yellow ochre in the center space at the top of your palette; this will be your only yellow. Place some black paint from a tube in the mixing area; add a small amount of ultramarine blue; mix well and test a sample of it with white to see that it is a low-key blue. (Do not use pure ultramarine blue in this triad.) Place the low-key blue in the blue space at the top of your palette; this will be your only blue.

Now mix the secondary colors. Combine the burnt sienna and yellow ochre to make the orange of this triad. Combine the yellow ochre and

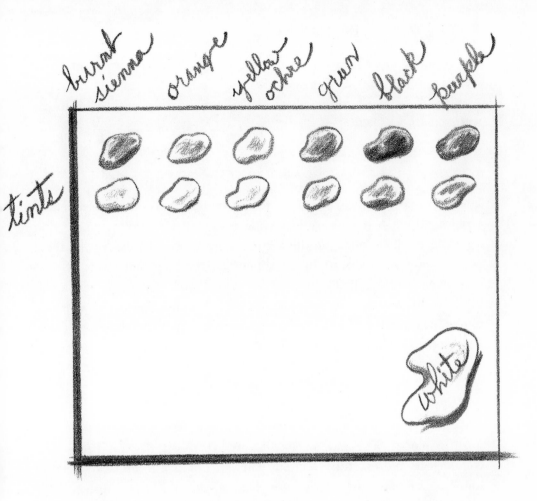

low-key blue to make the green. Combine the low-key blue and burnt sienna to make the purple. Remember to clean the mixing area after blending each of the secondary colors.

These secondary colors may seem rather dull on your palette, but the orange and yellow will be quite brilliant on your canvas. The green is a very subtle color, and the dark greens have a distinct richness. The purple may appear to be an almost neutral gray, but tints of this color will be a true violet-purple when placed on the canvas.

Make at least two tints of each of the six colors, one a very light tint and the other a value five.

Although this is a low-key triad, the warm colors—burnt sienna, orange and yellow ochre—can be improved by graying slightly. Burnt sienna used pure on the canvas is somewhat sharp and disagreeable; it can be made more pleasing by graying it slightly with a green of a five value.

The light and middle values of the low-key blue relate well to the warm colors.

ASSIGNMENT 1

Use a stretched canvas 30 by 32 inches or larger. Your brushes should be a least three inches across the ferrule.

The student tends to think immediately of a landscape in these colors, but you will learn more about this triad by first doing a non-objective painting. Paint hard-edge vertical and horizontal rectangles of different widths and lengths, combined with circles and parts of circles. The circles should not be lines—they should be shapes of color. Use a low-key white as one of your colors.

ASSIGNMENT 2

Now you can paint a landscape. In these colors landscapes are frequently moody and sad, even desolate. However, if you keep your colors clean and carefully related, you can produce a landscape that is quiet and serene. Use a large stretched canvas and large brushes.

HIGH-KEY TRIAD

The colors produced from a high-key triad serve an entirely different purpose. The colors can be brilliant and spectacular, or made luminous by graying. For this palette the colors are thalo red rose, cadmium yellow medium and thalo blue.

The name "thalo" appears on the tube of paint as "phthalocyanine blue," which is the correct name. Most painters use "thalo." Thalo blue and thalo green are colors of great brilliance on the canvas. Their pigment strength is dynamite. Thalo reds, however, are pigments of great beauty but average strength.

Experiment with thalo colors before you use them in a painting.

Since most of the thalo colors are unusually strong pigment colors, be aware that you will need very small amounts in mixtures with cadmium yellows.

Place the red, yellow and blue at the top of your palette in their respective places. Combine the red and yellow for orange, and set it up in the orange space. Be sure to clean the mixing area carefully for this triad—its success demands that each color division be very accurate. Combine cadmium yellow medium and thalo blue for an exciting green. Combine thalo blue and thalo red rose for a purple. Set the secondary colors in their places at the top of your palette.

For this series of colors it is important that you mix the interval colors, which can be done as you mix the secondaries. These colors are pure and very strong, and are quite beautiful: RO, OY, YG, GB, BP and RP. Make tints, about a four value, of each of the twelve colors; gray the tints.

Now gray the twelve pure colors with their complementary pure colors, and see how rich these forty-eight colors are—all from three tubes of paint. It is not necessary to use all these colors in one painting.

ASSIGNMENT 1

Use a large canvas, approximately 34 by 40 inches, and large brushes.

Paint a picture advertising a county fair or a carnival. Make the colors shrill and arresting. Do not depend on human figures for the action; let the shapes, values and color relationships tell the story.

ASSIGNMENT 2

On a canvas the size of your own choosing, paint a picture which reflects your feeling about these high-key colors.

Information Briefs

PAINT EMOTIONALLY

An uninvolved approach is evident to the observer. Paint emotionally. If you do not care greatly about your subject matter, how can the observer be moved by your painting? The world is constantly changing as you grow in knowledge and painting ability. Let your work reflect it. Don't remain static; it is as dangerous to copy your own successful painting as it is to copy the work of another artist.

Don't tell a story. If you must tell one, do it with pen and ink in prose or poetry.

Paint the things you know. If you enjoy painting trees, rocks and streams, go on field trips and get acquainted with them. Don't try to paint from memory the spot you saw last summer on your vacation, or the lovely place you saw in Maine eight years ago.

If you live in the city, paint the color and sound of the city. Don't paint every window in a skyscraper. You can express the excitement of the city by dramatic color and by the scale of your drawing.

In the country, if you paint a sawmill, convey the activity—the smell of the clean wood and the screaming of the saws. Make those who view your painting feel it.

And the sea—to paint it well you must live with it, if only for a few hours at a time. You must know the sea when the sun is shining on the rocks and turning the color of the water to pale green. You must know it in the roar of a storm when the wind sends the surf crashing on the rocks.

HOW BLUE IS THE SKY?

Think of the sky as a great bowl surrounding the earth. Do not paint it as if it were a flat backdrop for a theater stage. If it is to be a blue sky, let's make a mechanical analysis of the blues which might give the effect of a bowl.

Begin by taking a look at the sky directly overhead, where the blue is most intense. Let's say it is a strong tint of ultramarine blue. As your eye travels downward the blue gradually becomes lighter and becomes a tint of cobalt blue. It continues to lighten and warms up to a tint of cerulean blue. As it nears the earth a very light tint of blue-green appears, perhaps a tint of viridian. Close to the earth there is an area which is a light violet, or grayed violet. This effect is caused by the atmospheric dust from the earth. The violet made by a combination of cadmium red light and ultramarine blue has an earthy quality which gives the impression of distance. A violet color made from a combination of alizarin crimson and ultramarine blue has, at times, an artificial appearance. The style of your painting will dictate your choice.

Your painting may not demand all of these changes, but it is well to know exactly what part of the sky belongs in your painting.

Blue skies are great, but don't let them become a habit. A sky can be any color you happen to need for your picture to work. The bowl idea holds true for any color sky—go from cool to warm in sequence. A sky also changes in value from side to side, as it is slightly darker on the side away from the sun.

FLOWER PAINTING

Flower painting is a rich field. Consider the paintings of Matisse, Renoir, Monet, and more recently the paintings of Nicolai Fechin.

Here are a few ideas and suggestions—mostly "don'ts," I'm afraid.

A bouquet of flowers is a structure—it is three-dimensional. With brush and thin paint sketch a profile of the bouquet, indicating the amount of space it will occupy on the canvas. Mark the placement of the bowl or container, its height and width. Analyze the negative or air spaces around the subject. Don't let the container or bowl take up too much space and don't let it sit on the bottom edge of the canvas.

Think of the bouquet as an umbrella, the flowers at the center front are facing you and are nearest to you. The flowers to the left and right of center gradually face sideways. They also face slightly upward and become smaller toward the top. Don't draw all the flowers the same size and facing forward like polka dots.

If you were to paint a large bright pink flower at the center front near the bowl, and a flower of the same size and color at the top of the bouquet, the one at the top will appear larger and more brilliant than the lower one. It will also appear to fall forward. This illusion is the same as the one which requires that a framing mat on a watercolor painting be wider at the bottom than at the top.

Draw shapes containing several blossoms so that you have patterns of light and dark, as well as areas of the middle values.

The background should indicate that the flowers are surrounded by air and light. Establish the colors of the wall or the draperies behind the bouquet as you paint the flowers. These color relationships must proceed together. If flowers are painted against the white canvas, there can be no other background but white.

Do not complete the petals of the flowers until the very last— and don't paint every petal on every flower.

Finally, when you have decided on the mechanical structure of your picture, relax and paint the flowers as living things: the buds, the

half-blown flowers and the flowers in full bloom. This is the life cycle
—birth, youth and age.

BLACK

Black is unique; it is itself a color while at the same time it contains
all colors. There is much to learn about black, its possibilities and
limitations, its use and misuse, its power to enhance or to destroy. We
have already produced a black by mixing red, yellow and blue. That
was a semi-opaque black because red is an opaque color, yellow is slightly
opaque, and ultramarine blue is transparent.

Many of the commercial brands of tube black paint appear to be
true black. If tested by mixing with white, however, they produce blue-
grays. This means that they are intensely dark blues, and are cool colors.
The eye focuses on these colors and they seem to be farther away than
they actually are. Sometimes an area of tube black paint in a painting
does not appear on the same plane as the other colors; it seems to be
farther away.

Many painters "gray" their colors with black from a tube. The result is not the same as graying the colors with their complementaries. If
you gray a cadmium red light with black from a tube, you produce a
dark purple because you have really mixed red and blue. The vibrating
effect of yellow would be absent. In a similar way, if you gray a yellow
with black from a tube, the color you produce is green, not a grayed
yellow. Again the vibrating effect of red would be absent.

Black does have a charming neutralizing effect when mixed with
any color, but it is not the same as graying the color with its complementary.

Black is an excellent color to use for glazing. Sometimes an area
of several colors which seems too bright for the picture can be glazed
with black. It has the ability to unify the group or "pull it together."

Any red plus any yellow plus any dark blue will make a black.
Cerulean blue and some cobalts are not dark enough in value to make
a deep black. Some combinations of two colors may also make black;
burnt sienna and ultramarine blue makes a black because the burnt sienna

contains some yellow. Carmine and a very small amount of thalo green make a transparent black. Alizarin crimson and viridian make a type of black.

A large area of vibrating black can be produced by applying several dark (nine value) transparent colors directly to the canvas, overlapping slightly but not blending.

Do some experimenting on your own to discover which combinations of colors make transparent and which make opaque blacks.

Lesson 8:
An Expanded Triad

So far we have studied triads composed of only one red, one yellow and one blue. The student is now ready to gain control of the more complex expanded triad. The same procedure should be followed as was used in the Common Triad; however, we now use two or more reds, yellows or blues. We may use many reds, and only one yellow and one blue. Any combination of reds, yellows and blues is possible. Your selection of colors is governed by the color requirements of the subject you have chosen for your painting.

The need to relate the several colors in your painting now becomes evident; an unrelated color in a painting is as disturbing to the viewer as an off-color thread in a fine fabric. Colors are "woven" into a painting as an artist weaves colored threads into a tapestry.

Red and yellow are related by the color orange; yellow and blue by the color green, and blue and red by the color purple. To "relate" a color in an expanded triad means that each of the additional colors, red for instance, must be accompanied in a painting by an area, however small, of one or both of its secondaries—orange and/or purple.

If the orange secondary is used, it may be pure orange, a tint of orange or a grayed orange.

If the purple secondary is chosen, it may be any variation of red-purple, purple or blue-purple.

The secondary may appear anywhere on the canvas. Repetition of any color—in this instance red—is pleasing to the eye, which picks up its vibration even in the mixture of red and yellow called orange. In the same way, the eye picks up the vibration of yellow in the colors orange and green, and the vibration of blue in its secondaries, green and purple.

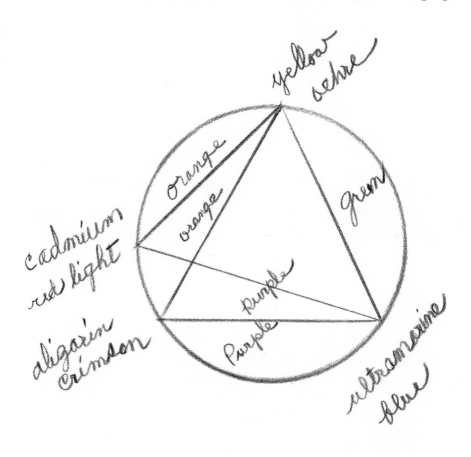

For the first expanded triad I have selected two reds, cadmium red light and alizarin crimson; one yellow, yellow ochre; and one blue, ultramarine blue.

This lesson not only increases the number of red pigment colors in our triad, it also expands the student's knowledge of the way the reds differ from each other. In painting a picture the student must experiment in the use of warm reds against cool reds, pure reds against grayed reds, and the use of tints of warm reds and tints of cool reds.

Although red colors will dominate in your painting, the color structure is still a triad pattern. Therefore the yellow and blue in their various forms will be needed to complete the composition.

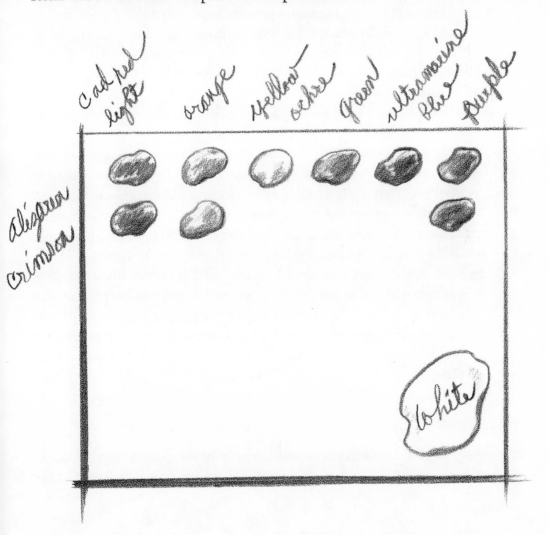

At the top of your palette on the left, place the two reds, one below the other. Place the yellow and blue in their usual spaces.

Mix one secondary orange by combining cadmium red light with yellow ochre. Mix the other secondary orange by combining alizarin crimson with yellow ochre. Place the two orange secondaries, one below the other, in the orange area at the top of your palette. Though these colors may seem almost alike, they will appear somewhat different on the canvas. This is especially true of their tints.

There will be only one green secondary in this pattern because there is only one yellow and only one blue. Place the green in its space at the top of your palette.

There will be two purples because there are two reds. Mix one purple by combining cadmium red light with ultramarine blue. Mix the other purple by combining alizarin crimson with ultramarine blue. Test a sample of each of these purples before placing them at the top of your palette, one below the other.

Now you have nine beautiful colors, two of red, two of orange, one yellow, one green, one blue and two of purple.

Before you make tints and before you make any grayed colors, you must decide which of the grays and tints you will need for your painting. By the time you might make tints of the nine colors, grayed the pure colors and grayed the tints, to say nothing of the interval colors, you would understand what an endless variety of colors can be produced by simply adding one red to a triad. With the experience you have gained in the previous lessons, you can now do some graying of the colors on your canvas as you paint, instead of mixing them on your palette. It is at this time that you realize the importance of visualizing color—seeing the exact color in your mind. If you have visualized color as you progressed through the lessons, your selection of tints and grayed colors will be simplified.

ASSIGNMENT

On a large stretched canvas with large brushes, paint a city landscape of buildings at close range. I suggest that you go take a walk and make several pencil sketches of buildings. The buildings should occupy most of the canvas, the sky a small area and the foreground a minimal area. Make a drawing with a brush dipped in lightly colored thinner. It can be made from a single sketch or a composite using more than one sketch to set up a good composition. The separation of buildings can be achieved by differences in values—some light buildings, some dark and others half-tones. Note the age of the buildings, the worn quality of the materials, and the sagging aspect of windows and trim.

This can be a city landscape, or a study of any site where a group of buildings pile up and make an interesting shape.

Lesson 9:
More Expanded Triads

Let's plan three new expanded triads: one for landscapes, one for flowers, and one for a large nonobjective painting or a very abstract floral composition.

For these triads the canvas should be at least 36 by 40 inches or 40 by 45 inches. I prefer that a large canvas be squarish. If you like a rectangular canvas, your choice could be 30 by 40 inches.

For the landscape triad I suggest burnt sienna (one red), cadmium yellow medium and yellow ochre (two yellows), and cerulean blue, viridian and ultramarine blue (three blues). I am considering viridian as a blue.

Place the burnt sienna in the red space at the top of your palette. Place the yellows, one below the other, in the yellow area. Place the blues, one below the other, in the blue area at the top of your palette. Mix the secondaries; you will have two orange secondaries, six greens and three purples. Make small amounts of the greens to determine which

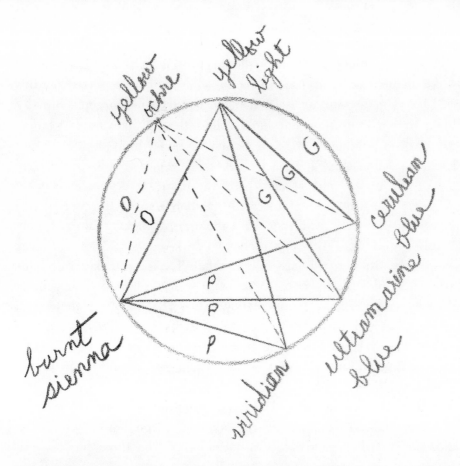

ones will be useful in your painting. You can always mix more of those needed to cover large areas. Be sure to clean the mixing area after each secondary.

If your landscape includes trees and shrubbery you may need the interval colors yellow-green, blue-green and perhaps red-purple. Before you put paint on your canvas, explore the many variations of these colors. Light tints of burnt sienna appear as natural pinks in a green landscape. These combined with tints of red-purple are effective. Rust colors may be developed by graying the middle tints of burnt sienna with greens. Dark greens may be grayed with burnt sienna and light greens with a tint of burnt sienna. The purple secondaries will be low-key and useful in a landscape. Gray them slightly for soil, old wood and rocks. The purple made of ultramarine blue and burnt sienna will be almost pure black. Try graying the orange with blue-purple (instead of blue) or a tint of blue-purple—it works better in a landscape.

Use pure orange and pure yellow sparingly in a landscape unless you are doing a brilliant autumn scene, which is not suggested for this triad. When your painting is finshed, do not try to "sharpen it up" by adding strokes of brilliant unrelated color—those strokes never become a part of the painting, but seem always to be in front of the picture plane. Paint a fine landscape.

For the flower triad let us expand the reds. Make your own circle and palette diagrams. I suggest an expanded triad of three reds, two yellows and one blue. The reds are cadmium red light, thalo red rose, and alizarin crimson. Although these two dark reds appear very similar as they come from the tube, their tints differ. Thalo red makes a brilliant warm pink, and alizarin crimson makes a very cool pink. The yellows will be cadmium yellow light and yellow ochre. The one blue is thalo blue.

Place the reds, one below the other, at the top of your palette on the left. Place the yellows, one below the other, in the yellow area. Place the blue toward the right, leaving room for the many purple secondaries.

The reds must be related in your painting by their secondaries. The orange may be made from the reds mixed with either or both of the yellows. You will have two green secondaries. The three purples and their tints will be most useful in a flower painting. Because of the delicate variations in the colors of flowers, you may need the interval colors: RO, OY, YG, BG, BP and RP. These colors may be mixed as you need them.

Remember that bright colors do not make a bright painting; it is the juxtaposition of the warm and cool colors which causes vibration and brilliance.

By now you should be able to mix some of the colors on your canvas. Eventually, when the color combinations become a habit, you will find flexibility and freedom this way.

ASSIGNMENT 1

Paint a nonobjective painting with each of these palettes of expanded triads. These should be done on large canvases—nothing less than 30 inches in both dimensions.

ASSIGNMENT 2

Paint a nonobjective painting or an abstract landscape with the first triad. Use large brushes on a large canvas. Try to give it the "feel" of the outdoors without painting every tree and every rock.

With the second expanded triad paint a nonobjective painting on a large canvas, using very large brushes. Suggest the feeling of flowers without painting each blossom, stem and leaf. Paint shapes with some quiet spaces.

For the third expanded triad I will suggest the colors and give no further directions. You should be able to set up your palette carefully, explore the possibilities of these colors, and proceed with the necessary secondaries, tints and grayed colors.

The colors are two reds: acra red and thalo red rose; three yellows: cadmium yellow light, yellow ochre and zinc yellow; and two blues: thalo blue and tube black.

This is essentially a triad with emphasis on yellow. Don't forget that orange and yellow-green are also yellows.

Lesson Nine provides students with an opportunity to increase the variety and richness of the color in their paintings—this time by concentration on the color blue in its variations of blue pigment tube colors.

ASSIGNMENT 3

With large brushes on a large canvas, paint a nonobjective or an abstract painting. Paint shapes, not things. Large areas of what we sometimes term muddy colors can be made to glow when opposed by smaller areas of brilliant color and quiet spaces. Take plenty of time for this one.

65243

Information Briefs

THE USES OF PAINTING MEDIUM

Students often say to me, "Everyone gives a formula for painting medium, but no one tells us why, when or how to use it."

The painting media have been discussed in the chapter on Materials. Here I will remind the reader that the term medium has several meanings. First it is the material with which the artist chooses to work. A second meaning is that of a solvent for paint. The third meaning is: a solution of three ingredients, varnish, oil and turpentine, mixed according to a long-established formula.

As early as the thirteenth century, the Dutch painters used copal varnish, stand oil and rectified turpentine as a painting medium. This medium preserved their paintings against the dampness of the climate. Even today this is an excellent formula.

A popular formula now is one-third Damar varnish, one-third linseed oil and one-third turpentine (or paint thinner). Many artists use this formula because they prefer a dull or "matte" finish on their paintings.

Damar varnish is available in a matte finish as well as a gloss finish; copal varnish comes in a gloss finish only. When the three ingredients have been measured into a container, they should be stirred carefully. Never shake the container, as this causes minute air bubbles to form in the varnish. The bubbles may not break until they reach the surface of the painting, leaving tiny "bubble marks."

When I prepare the formula containing linseed oil, I reduce the amount of the oil by one-half to facilitate drying since this oil dries very slowly.

One use of the painting-medium formula is to extend the paint by permitting it to flow more freely. It gives a rich glossy quality to the paint, due to the varnish which the medium contains. Some artists use the medium as they paint, dipping into it with their brush as the water-color painter dips into water. The danger, however, is that the paint may be diluted too much. It loses the richness that an oil painting should have and the painting becomes a series of washes. I urge the beginning painter to use the paint as it comes directly from the tube in order to become accustomed to the texture and beauty of oil paint.

The painting-medium formula is also used for repainting. A fine oil painting is seldom accomplished in a single session; it is sometimes necessary to let areas dry before continuing. If a few days have elapsed since a painting session, and the paint on your canvas has started to "set," do not paint into it with fresh paint, but allow it to dry completely before going on. As the paint dries, a skin or smooth surface forms. Then the impurities in the air settle on this surface and form an invisible, but none the less real, scum on the paint. The next layer of paint may seem to adhere, but might at some future time flake off in spots.

To prevent this separation, brush on a very thin coat of painting medium diluted with turpentine or paint thinner before you continue painting. This will create a bond between the layers of paint. Start at the top of the canvas and use a very clean brush which has been dipped in diluted medium. Draw a brush stroke across the canvas slowly. The second stroke should overlap the first. Continue overlapping strokes until the bottom of the canvas is reached and the whole canvas is covered.

Use no more medium than is absolutely necessary. Tilt the canvas slightly to be sure that there are no drips. Start painting immediately into the moistened surface of the canvas.

The use of the painting medium is also important in the process of glazing, which is described next.

GLAZING

A glaze is a very thin layer of transparent color, or colors, superimposed on a dry painting. The paint is made very thin by the addition of diluted painting medium. If varnish is used for glazing and several different color glazes are needed—one on top of the other—the varnish will make the surface of the canvas brittle and subject to cracking. The painting-medium formula, being a mixture of varnish, oil and turpentine (or thinner), gives more flexibility to the surface of the canvas.

In simple terms, glazing is the refinement of color in a painting. It is used in many ways. Glaze can be used to enrich certain colors or a group of colors. By glazing, a shift of emphasis may be achieved, reducing the importance of some areas and increasing the importance of others. An overall glaze with one color may give an "atmosphere" to a whole painting.

A glaze may be used to deepen a color on the canvas, such as a thin layer of alizarin crimson over a cadmium red light. The color remains red but gains new depth and richness. A glaze may change the color entirely. Placing a very thin layer of ultramarine blue over an area of yellow causes the yellow to become green. By placing a thin layer of black over an area of yellow, the yellow again turns green but it is a strange, grayed green. A good way to discover the unusual colors created by glazing is to experiment on your own discarded canvases.

I prefer to do the glazing process with the painting lying almost horizontally on a table. If a canvas is raised only five or six inches at the top edge, the painting medium will not move too rapidly down the surface.

Here is the technique to change some of the colors in a completely dry painting, while keeping other colors as they are. Choose the colors you wish to use for each color change, and place a small amount of these colors on your palette, widely separated.

With a brushful of colorless diluted medium, start at the top on the left and draw a stroke slowly across the painting. Your second stroke should overlap the first. Be sure that there are no drips. Continue down the canvas until you reach the area which needs a change of color. Pick up a small amount of the glazing color and work it into your brush on the palette, using plenty of the medium. Cover the area with the color until you have the desired deepened color. Rinse the color from your brush and wipe dry. Cover the remaining canvas with the transparent medium until you reach another spot which needs a change of color. Several different areas can be changed in color in one operation. When you have reached the bottom of the canvas, check to see that there are no dry spots.

One small area alone cannot be glazed without working through the above process because the glazed area would be the only shiny spot on the painting.

Some artists glaze using turpentine or paint thinner instead of the painting-medium formula. These solutions are unsatisfactory because they cannot hold the grains of pigment in suspension. I find all the color at the bottom of my canvas.

If you wish to make further changes, more than one glaze may be applied, allowing complete drying time between each glazing. It is well to note that each time a color is applied over another color, the area becomes darker.

Historically, glazing was done with transparent colors only. Today we are not so restrictive, and some beautiful and unusual color changes can be produced by glazing with some of the opaque colors.

WARM AND COOL COLORS

Some of the artists' colors are of ancient origin. As long ago as 4000 B. C., the Egyptians, the first color-makers, produced azurite and malachite, a blue and a green, from copper. From a pottery glaze, they made Alexandria blue; from cinnabar, a vermilion; and from arsenic a yellow called orpiment that is similar to our yellow ochre. Reds and pinks were extracted from madder root.

About 2500 B. C. color-making passed to Greece, where many of the colors were perfected, particularly vermilion. The Greeks learned distilling, and through this process made fine varnishes by combining the drying oils—linseed, walnut and poppy—with mastic or sanderac.

Later, the Italians contributed the earth colors—siennas, umbers, yellow ochre and Naples yellow, a lead material from the slopes of Mount Vesuvius. Early in the Renaissance period a magnificent ultramarine blue was made from lapis lazuli. Although only the jewelers' cuttings were used, the color was too costly for general use. Cobalt came from the mines in Saxony, and viridian from Africa. Cadmium yellow and cadmium red were made from minerals mined in Australia.

It was not until the advent of scientific chemistry in 1820 that ultramarine blue, as we know it, was produced, followed by chrome green and yellow oxide.

Several pinks and reds called "lake" colors were produced from coal tar about 1890. Of these, only alizarin crimson was a permanent color.

About 1930, new colors called phthalocyanine, or "thalo," colors, appeared in our stores. They were a transparent blue and green of great brilliance, followed by a series of cool transparent reds and an opaque yellow-green. These are our most recent color discoveries.

Warm colors bring to mind the colors of fire—the reds and yellows. Cool colors make us think of the blue of the sky, of water and ice.

As the paint comes from the tube, some reds are warm and some are cool. On the canvas the temperature of a color depends on the colors which surround it. Alizarin crimson is cool when placed against cadmium red light; but it is warm against a grayed green.

In the same way, some yellows are warm and some are cool. Zinc yellow, when placed beside cadmium yellow light, seems to recede— it is cool. However, when placed beside a violet-purple, it is warm. Ultramarine blue seems cool when placed beside cerulean blue, but it has a purplish quality which makes it warm beside a thalo blue. Titanium white is warm, compared with zinc white which is cool. Since white is a neutralizing color, any color mixed with white becomes less warm.

Here is a list of permanent colors available in any of the well-known brands. It is not a complete list of all colors, but includes the basic colors, long used and recognized. From this list of colors, make your selections for new triads and expanded triads.

WARM REDS
Cadmium red light
Cadmium red medium
Cadmium red deep
Vermilion
Acra red
Carmine
Burnt sienna

COOL REDS
Alizarin crimson
Rose madder
Thalo red rose
Venetian red
Indian red
Light red

WARM YELLOWS
Cadmium yellow light
Cadmium yellow medium
Cadmium yellow deep
Naples yellow
Raw sienna
Cadmium orange

COOL YELLOWS
Cadmium yellow pale
Lemon yellow
Zinc yellow
Raw umber
Yellow ochre

WARM BLUES
Ultramarine blue
Cobalt blue
Cerulean blue
Permanent green light
Thalo yellow green
Cobalt violet
Ivory black

COOL BLUES
Prussian blue
Thalo blue
Viridian green
Lamp black

WARM WHITE
Titanium white

COOL WHITE
Zinc white

TRANSPARENT AND OPAQUE COLORS

Colors are either transparent or opaque to a degree. One can see through transparent color as if seeing through colored glass. Opaque color is dense or impenetrable to the eye. It covers the surface, you cannot see through it.

Colors which are transparent in oil paint are also transparent in watercolor paint and acrylic paint. And colors which are opaque in oils are opaque in watercolors and acrylics. Recently, a transparent color belonging to the "yellow family" was made available in acrylic paint. There are no true transparent yellows in oil paint.

White is an opaque color. Any color, even a transparent color, if mixed with white becomes opaque.

TRANSPARENT COLORS	OPAQUE COLORS
Alizarin crimson	Cadmium red light
Rose madder	Cadmium red medium
Thalo red rose	Cadmium red deep
Acra red	Vermilion
Carmine	Venetian red
Burnt sienna	Indian red
Ultramarine blue	Light red
Prussian blue	Cadmium yellow light
Cobalt blue	Cadmium yellow medium
Thalo blue	Cadmium yellow deep
Thalo green	Yellow ochre
Viridian green	Naples yellow
Raw umber	Cadmium orange
Ivory black	Cadmium yellow pale
	Lemon yellow
	Zinc yellow
	Thalo yellow green
	Cerulean blue

Zinc white
Titanium white
Mars black
Lamp black

Traditionally, only transparent color was used for glazing. The small jewel-like paintings of the thirteenth century were made by superimposing glazes of transparent color on a picture painted in values of gray on a white base of egg tempera. Since texture is important in nonobjective paintings, glazing with opaque color is now frequently used. A glaze made by combining an opaque color with the painting medium leaves a thin film of grainy color (texture) on the surface of the area glazed.

INTRODUCING ANALOGOUS COLOR

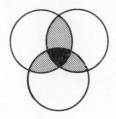

An Explanation

We will leave the triad pattern of color for a new color pattern called analogous color. Analogous is defined as related, or comparable in certain respects. In painting, analogous color means colors belonging to the same color family and adjacent to each other on the color wheel.

All colors containing red belong to the same color family and are analogous to each other. In the same way, all colors containing yellow are analogous, and those colors containing blue are analogous. A painting made up of all red color would not seem complete because the eye demands all the colors in white light: red, yellow and blue. Therefore, in a red analogous pattern at least one green complementary will be needed to complete the color pattern. In a yellow analogous pattern at least one purple color will be needed, and in a blue analogous pattern at least one orange color will be needed.

The basic difference between the triad color pattern and the analogous color pattern is that in the triad pattern (including all tints), each color has its own complementary and is grayed by its own comple-mentary color. In the analogous pattern, the complementary of one of the colors is selected, and that color is used as the only complementary. All colors are grayed by that one complementary color.

The arrangement of colors in the analogous pattern facilitates closer color relationships. Since the study of color is expressly for the purpose of producing greater variety, richness and beauty, the analogous pattern introduces to the artist-painter a new color attitude.

Lesson 10:
Analogous Color-Yellow

There are many possible groups of analogous colors, but for this lesson I have selected four colors which are related to the color yellow. The four analogous colors for this pattern will be orange, orange-yellow, yellow and yellow-green. To produce the four analogous colors we will use the three primary tube colors: cadmium red light, cadmium yellow light and ultramarine blue. These are my selections; later you may wish to substitute the different tube colors which are analogous: cadmium yellow light, cadmium yellow medium, cadmium yellow deep, yellow ochre, Naples yellow, raw sienna, Indian yellow, zinc yellow and others.

In order to understand and visualize these colors, draw your color wheel. Locate the red, yellow and blue and then the secondaries; orange, green and purple. Next mark off the intervals: red-orange, orange-yellow, yellow-green, green-blue, blue-purple and red-purple.

Draw a line from the center of the circle to each of the four analogous colors: orange, orange-yellow, yellow and yellow-green.

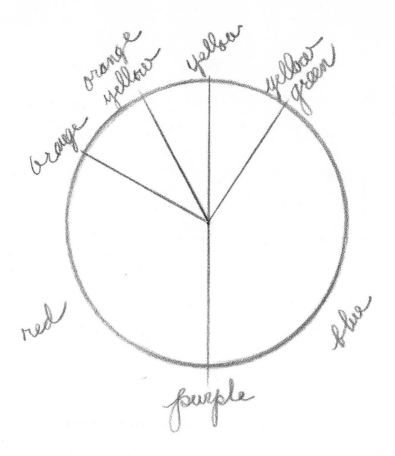

We have already learned that the eye demands all the colors in white light. With these four analogous colors we have a large amount of yellow, a small amount of red, and a very small amount of blue. In order to arrive at a pleasant balance of color, and to give our painting a sense of completeness, we need the complementary of *one* of our analogous colors. For this lesson I have selected purple as the one complementary. Draw a line from the center of the circle to the purple complementary. Later you may choose to select one of the other complementaries.

There will be a new arrangement of colors at the top of your palette. The primary colors red, yellow and blue will be used in the mixing area only. For analogous color lessons there will be only five colors at the top of the palette; the analogous colors will occupy the first four spaces and the fifth will be for the complementary color, purple.

First mix some yellow with a bit of red to make orange. Set it up

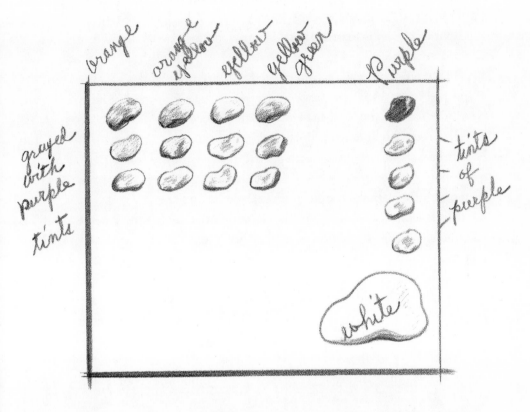

at the top of the palette on the left. Since you will need a quantity of color for this lesson, be generous as you mix.

In the mixing area now place some yellow, to which you will add a smaller amount of red to make an orange-yellow. Be sure that there is a clear difference between this color and orange. Place it at the top of your palette in the second space.

The third color is yellow, so squeeze out some yellow directly from the tube into the third place at the top of your palette.

Finally, after cleaning the mixing area, squeeze out some more yellow in the mixing area, to which you will add a bit of blue to make a yellow-green. Be sure it is a yellow-green, not a green. Set it up at the top of your palette in the fourth place.

Mix the purple from cadmium red light and ultramarine blue. Do not mix a large amount. Make a test of a bit of it to be sure that it is not a blue-purple nor a red-purple. Purple will then occupy the upper right corner of the palette.

Our next step is to relate the four analogous colors to the one complementary—purple.

Place half the orange color in the mixing area. Add a small amount of purple to it until you have a beautiful dark brown. If the mixture is not a rich dark brown, it may be that the orange is not quite red enough. Set the brown up at the top of the palette just below the orange.

Take half of the yellow-orange and place it in the mixing area. Add a very small amount of purple until you have a light golden brown. Set it up under the yellow-orange and clean the mixing area.

Place half the yellow in the mixing area and add a very small amount of purple. It should look like "green-gold." If you use too much purple, you cannot get this color. Set it up below the yellow at the top of your palette.

Finally, mix the last color by taking half the yellow-green and placing it in the mixing area. Add some purple and you should have a dark muddy green. Set it up under the yellow-green.

Make tints of the four colors just mixed. The first two should be warm colors—the browns. The next two should be cool colors—the greens. Make at least three tints of the purple. Very light tints of all these colors are beautiful neutrals.

In this color pattern remember you are going to explore all the possibilities of yellow. So don't start using large areas of the pure purples for your darks. You have a handsome dark golden brown and a fine muddy green for this purpose.

The tints of purple may be used to enhance the other combinations of yellow. In this assignment feel free to use your four original analogous colors as well as their tints. You may also use white.

ASSIGNMENT

The colors you have just mixed almost demand an autumn landscape. Make this your first assignment.

When you have finished the landscape, do a nonobjective painting with these colors. Try to express the same feeling which the observer would experience upon viewing the landscape.

Lesson 11:
Analogous Color-Red

The color pattern in this lesson is made up of various red pigment tube colors. The compound colors produced are quite different from those in the expanded red triad. Each change in color arrangement, color quantity or complementary color produces a result different from that of any other combination.

Draw a color wheel indicating the primary colors, the secondary colors and the intervals, marking them with the initials R, RO, O, OY and so on.

From this wheel I will select four colors related to each other by the color red. Later you may wish to make a slightly different selection. The analogous colors this time are red-purple, red, red-orange and orange. Draw lines from the center of the color wheel to each of the four chosen colors. The next step is to select the complementary color of one of these reds. The choice is from the following: yellow-green, green, blue-green and blue. Yellow-green is rather warm for the warm red

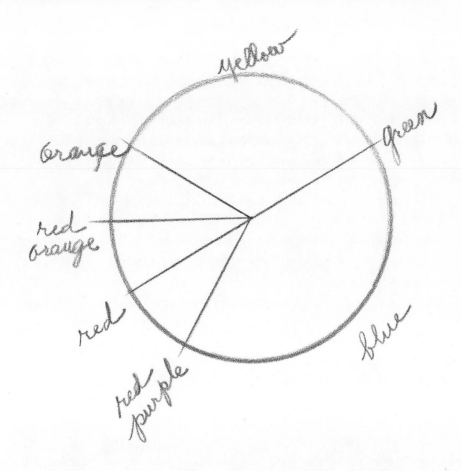

palette, and since blue-green and blue are almost too dark in value, I have decided on green. Draw a line from the center of the circle to the color green.

Now that you have observed the location of our analogous colors on the wheel, you will proceed to substitute pigment tube colors for the basic colors of red-purple, red, red-orange and orange.

Make a red-purple by combining ultramarine blue with alizarin crimson. Set it up at the top of the palette in the first space on the left. For the analogous color red, I suggest the tube color acra red. Squeeze some acra red into the second space at the top of the palette.

For the third color, red-orange, I suggest you use cadmium red light because in relation to the other reds, it becomes a red-orange. Squeeze some "red-orange" into the third space at the top of the palette. For the fourth color use a tube of orange. Squeeze some orange into the fourth space at the top of the palette. These colors are different from the colors which you might have produced from the primary colors, but the principle remains the same.

Now mix the complementary color green. Start with cadmium yellow light in the mixing area, and add a small amount of ultramarine blue to make a lively green. Set the green at the top of your palette in the fifth place.

Since these colors are rather dark in value, I suggest that you make a strong tint of each in order to observe the graying process. Place each tint under its respective color at the top of your palette.

The same procedure is followed as in the previous lesson. We relate a tint of each of the four analogous colors to the complementary green.

In discussing "Analogous Color—Yellow," each mixed color had a name, for example, dark brown, golden brown, green-gold and muddy green. The colors in this lesson are merely described as compound colors; there are no specific names to describe them.

Place half the tint of red-purple into the mixing area and add a small amount of the green complementary. Blend and set the mixed color below the tint of red-purple. Clean the mixing area.

Take half of the tint of acra red and place in the mixing area; add a small amount of the complementary, green. Set the mixture up under the tint of acra red. These first two compound colors should be somewhat cool. Experiment with various quantities of the complementary color.

Place half the red-orange (cadmium red light) in the mixing area and add some green. Place the mixture up under the tint of red-orange.

Place half the tint of orange in the mixing area, and combine with some green. Place this mixture under the tint of orange. These third and fourth mixtures should be quite warm.

Mix a tint of each of these grayed colors. Mix at least three tints of green.

Now gray a small amount of the pure dark colors with the pure green. Orange combined with green makes a handsome and flexible color.

In this palette remember that you are dealing with reds—don't be afraid of them. If you are doing an abstract landscape start by making

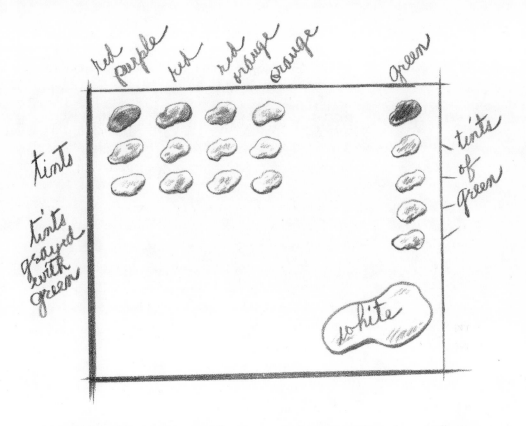

the sky red. Why not? There are many areas where the soil is red. There are red trees, red flowers, red coats, red balloons, red hair, red buildings, red cabbage! Reds are gorgeous.

ASSIGNMENT 1

Paint an abstract landscape with these colors. Don't forget to consider a red sky—or at least an orange-colored sky.

ASSIGNMENT 2

This will be an assignment of your own choosing. Be as original in the choice of subject matter as you are in the use of these colors.

Lesson 12:
Analogous Color-Blue

PART A

This lesson is presented in two parts, both dealing with the blue analogous colors: green, blue-green, blue and blue-purple. This first part analyzes colors made from the primary tube colors: cadmium red light, cadmium yellow light and ultramarine blue.

On your color wheel mark the primaries, secondaries and intervals indicating them by their initials. Draw lines from the center of the wheel to each of the colors: green, blue-green, blue and blue-purple.

I suggest orange for the complementary color to be shared by these four colors. Draw a line from the center of the wheel to the color orange to complete the color pattern.

In the mixing area place some yellow, adding enough blue to make a bright lively green. Keep it as light in value as possible. Place the green in the first space on the left side at the top of your palette.

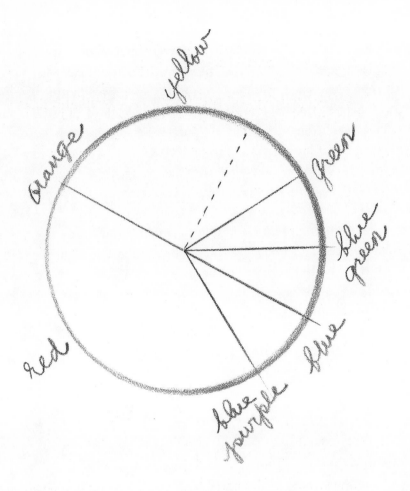

In the mixing area place some yellow, adding blue to make a blue-green. Test a small amount of the mixture with white to be sure that you have blue-green. Place it in the second space at the top of the palette. Clean the mixing area.

Since blue is our third color, squeeze some ultramarine blue from the tube into the third space at the top. Then place some blue in the mixing area, and add enough red to make a blue-purple. Make a test of a small amount with white to insure your having a blue-purple. Set it up in the fourth space at the top of your palette. Clean the mixing area.

To mix our complementary color orange, place some yellow in the mixing area and add a small amount of red. Be precise in mixing this color. There is a recognizable difference among the three gradations of orange: red-orange, orange and orange-yellow. If the orange you mix for this lesson is too yellow, all of your grayed colors will become greens. Set the mixed orange in the upper right corner of your palette.

All the colors are dark in value and, therefore, below the threshold of sight. I suggest that you mix a bright tint of each of the four related colors. Place each tint just below its pure color. Now you have tints of green, blue-green, blue and blue-purple.

In the mixing area take half the tint of green and add a bit of orange, enough to keep the mixture a warm green. Set this mixture up just below the tint of green.

Place half the tint of blue-green in the mixing area; add some orange. This color will be slightly cool. Set it up below the tint of blue-green.

Place half the tint of blue in the mixing area, adding some orange. If you add too much orange, the mixture will become green. Set it up below the tint of blue.

Place half the tint of blue-purple in the mixing area, adding a small amount of orange. The mixture should be slightly warm when compared to the blend made with blue. This mixture will be a dark brown.

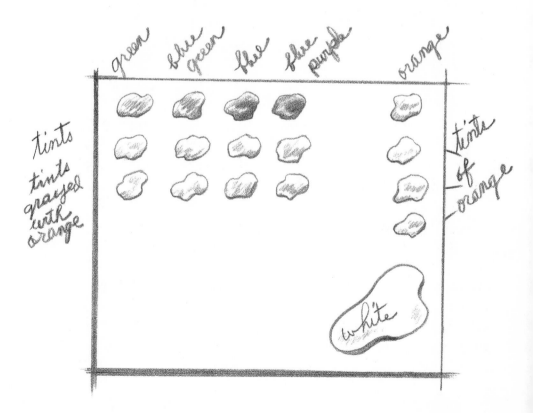

Mix many light tints of these colors. Students tend to make only dark tints of the cool colors, thereby missing their brilliance. Before you complete your palette, mix the four pure colors with orange, and you will find exciting, rich dark colors.

Make three tints of the orange complementary. Since this is a series of blue related colors, be sure that your painting is a blue one, not an orange one.

ASSIGNMENT 1

On a large canvas with large brushes paint a nonobjective picture. Although this is a cool palette, there are many colors which are relatively warm. Find the ones with depth. Use warm colors against cool colors. Some mixed colors which seem "muddy" on the palette become glowing areas when juxtaposed with smaller areas of bright, sparkling colors. Use the orange and its tints to accentuate the cool areas.

ASSIGNMENT 2

These colors bring to mind a seascape. You have an array of blues, greens and violets for the sea and sky. You also have a fine color for rocks and sand.

PART B

The second part of this lesson follows the same analogous color pattern, but we add one color and substitute tube colors.

Ordinarily no more than four colors are used in an analogous color pattern. Too many colors become a burden to mix. However, since the blue-related colors are so dark in value, we add the fifth color, yellow-green. This addition is pure color in light value. It is easy to get light values by adding white to any color, but these are never as brilliant as the pure-color light values. (When a series of colors includes two pure-color primaries, they are no longer an analogous color pattern; they automatically become a triad pattern.)

On your color wheel mark the primaries, secondaries and intervals. From the center of the wheel draw lines to the five colors: yellow-green, green, blue-green, blue and blue-purple. We will use the same shared complementary color, orange. So draw a line from the center to the color orange.

When substituting tube colors, you should first decide on the basic pure color. For this series of colors I suggest thalo blue. Yellow-green and green will be mixed by combining cadmium yellow light with very small amounts of thalo blue.

For the blue-green substitute cerulean blue. Purple will be a mixture of alizarin crimson and thalo blue.

Set up the five pure colors at the top of your palette, leaving room for the orange complementary. Make bright tints of the five colors, setting up each one just below its pure color at the top of the palette. Clean the palette after mixing each color.

Combine each of the tints with the orange to produce the many possible grayed colors. Mix small amounts of the pure colors with orange to find other rich dark colors.

Mix many very light tints of all of these handsome colors to develop beautiful warm and cool variations.

ASSIGNMENT

Do many paintings in this color pattern. The more hours you spend at your easel, the greater the progress you will make.

Afterword

When a student asks, "How do I become a successful artist?" I wonder what exactly to say. The artist's goal is to develop inborn creative ability. If the aim is to please relatives and astonish friends, or to make money, the artist will never reach creative heights.

In our present system it is often a good idea to enter paintings in juried shows. I am assuming that you are becoming competent in color, composition and drawing. Don't be discouraged if your paintings are not accepted at first. Over a period of time the jurors' evaluation of your work will be fairly accurate. Learn from these experiences.

A knowledge of art history is essential, so plan a program of reading. All art is a continuation of the art of the past. Each period has amplified the colors and techniques of preceeding eras, and in turn has left its own unique quality.

Your reading should start with paleolithic time and the paintings in the caves of France and Spain. Consider the art of West Africa as

117

well as that of Egypt. Move on through the periods of Greek, Byzantine, Roman and Renaissance art. Follow with the Impressionists and the Moderns. It is interesting to compare the art of England, Flanders, Holland and Germany from the thirteenth century on with that of the rest of Europe.

Visit museums and art galleries. See the originals of the "Old Masters," the Impressionists, and the work of artists of this century. Reproductions do not convey the richness and beauty of these paintings. Be aware of contemporary painting, especially that of the young painters who will be the important artists of tomorrow. At times when you cannot paint—read.

Finally there is only one real word of advice to give a student. It is, Paint! Paint constantly and paint regularly. Count your painting experience not by the number of years that you have been painting, but by the number of hours that you have spent at your easel. Count them as an airplane pilot numbers flying hours. The hours spent at your easel are the important ones.

Have a happy time painting!